VOLUME 632

NOVEMBER 2010

THE ANNALS

of The American Academy of Political
and Social Science

PHYLLIS KANISS, *Executive Editor*

Perspectives on Africa and the World

Special Editors:

TUKUFU ZUBERI
University of Pennsylvania

TANJI GILLIAM
University of Pennsylvania

Los Angeles | London | New Delhi
Singapore | Washington DC

Origin and Purpose. The Academy was organized December 14, 1889, to promote the progress of political and social science, especially through publications and meetings. The Academy does not take sides in controverted questions, but seeks to gather and present reliable information to assist the public in forming an intelligent and accurate judgment.

Meetings. The Academy occasionally holds a meeting in the spring extending over two days.

Publications. THE ANNALS of The American Academy of Political and Social Science is the bimonthly publication of the Academy. Each issue contains articles on some prominent social or political problem, written at the invitation of the editors. These volumes constitute important reference works on the topics with which they deal, and they are extensively cited by authorities throughout the United States and abroad.

Membership. Each member of the Academy receives THE ANNALS and may attend the meetings of the Academy. Membership is open only to individuals. Annual dues: $94.00 for the regular paperbound edition (clothbound, $134.00). Members may also purchase single issues of THE ANNALS for $18.00 each (clothbound, $27.00). Student memberships are available for $52.00.

Subscriptions. THE ANNALS of The American Academy of Political and Social Science (ISSN 0002-7162) (J295) is published bimonthly—in January, March, May, July, September, and November—by SAGE Publications, 2455 Teller Road, Thousand Oaks, CA 91320. Periodicals postage paid at Thousand Oaks, California, and at additional mailing offices. POSTMASTER: Send address changes to The Annals of The American Academy of Political and Social Science, c/o SAGE Publications, 2455 Teller Road, Thousand Oaks, CA 91320. Institutions may subscribe to THE ANNALS at the annual rate: $788.00 (clothbound, $889.00). Single issues of THE ANNALS may be obtained by individuals who are not members of the Academy for $142.00 each (clothbound, $160.00). Single issues of THE ANNALS have proven to be excellent supplementary texts for classroom use. Direct inquiries regarding adoptions to THE ANNALS c/o SAGE Publications (address below).

All correspondence concerning membership in the Academy, dues renewals, inquiries about membership status, and/or purchase of single issues of THE ANNALS should be sent to THE ANNALS c/o SAGE Publications, 2455 Teller Road, Thousand Oaks, CA 91320. Telephone: (800) 818-SAGE (7243) and (805) 499-0721; Fax/Order line: (805) 375-1700; e-mail: journals@sagepub.com. *Please note that orders under $30 must be prepaid.* For all customers outside the Americas, please visit http://www.sagepub.co.uk/customerCare.nav for information.

Printed on acid-free paper

THE ANNALS

© 2010 by The American Academy of Political and Social Science

Editorial Office: 202 S. 36th Street, Philadelphia, PA 19104-3806
For information about membership* (individuals only) and subscriptions (institutions), address:
SAGE Publications
2455 Teller Road
Thousand Oaks, CA 91320

For SAGE Publications: Allison Leung (Production) and Lori Hart (Marketing)

From India and South Asia,
write to:
SAGE PUBLICATIONS INDIA Pvt Ltd
B-42 Panchsheel Enclave, P.O. Box 4109
New Delhi 110 017
INDIA

From Europe, the Middle East,
and Africa, write to:
SAGE PUBLICATIONS LTD
1 Oliver's Yard, 55 City Road
London EC1Y 1SP
UNITED KINGDOM

*Please note that members of the Academy receive THE ANNALS with their membership.
International Standard Serial Number ISSN 0002-7162
International Standard Book Number ISBN 978-1-4129-9394-4 (Vol. 632, 2010) paper
International Standard Book Number ISBN 978-1-4129-9395-1 (Vol. 632, 2010) cloth
Manufactured in the United States of America. First printing, November 2010.

Please visit http://ann.sagepub.com and under the "More about this journal" menu on the right-hand side, click on the Abstracting/Indexing link to view a full list of databases in which this journal is indexed.

Information about membership rates, institutional subscriptions, and back issue prices may be found on the facing page.

Advertising. Current rates and specifications may be obtained by writing to The Annals Advertising and Promotion Manager at the Thousand Oaks office (address above). Acceptance of advertising in this journal in no way implies endorsement of the advertised product or service by SAGE or the journal's affiliated society(ies) or the journal editor(s). No endorsement is intended or implied. SAGE reserves the right to reject any advertising it deems as inappropriate for this journal.

Claims. Claims for undelivered copies must be made no later than six months following month of publication. The publisher will supply replacement issues when losses have been sustained in transit and when the reserve stock will permit.

Change of Address. Six weeks' advance notice must be given when notifying of change of address. Please send the old address label along with the new address to the SAGE office address above to ensure proper identification. Please specify the name of the journal.

THE ANNALS

OF THE AMERICAN ACADEMY OF POLITICAL AND SOCIAL SCIENCE

Volume 632   November 2010

IN THIS ISSUE:

Perspectives on Africa and the World

Special Editors: TUKUFU ZUBERI
TANJI GILLIAM

Introduction

A Perspective on Africa and the World . . . . *Tukufu Zuberi*   5

Black Africans in World War II:
  The Soldiers' Stories . . . . *John H. Morrow Jr.*   12

The Ogaden War and the Demise of Détente . . . . *Donna R. Jackson*   26

Decolonization or National Liberation: Debating
  the End of British Colonial Rule in Africa . . . . *Cheikh Anta Babou*   41

Radical Islam in East Africa . . . . *Charles R. Stith*   55

Debating Darfur in the World . . . . *Rogaia Mustafa Abusharaf*   67

The United States of Africa: A Revisit . . . . *George B. N. Ayittey*   86

Africa's Development beyond Aid:
  Getting Out of the Box . . . . *Julius Gatune*   103

Afrocentricity and the Argument for
  Civic Commitment: Ideology and Citizenship
  in a United States of Africa . . . . *Molefi Kete Asante*   121

Erratum   132

FORTHCOMING

The Child as Citizen

Special Editor: FELTON EARLS

A Perspective on Africa and the World

By
TUKUFU ZUBERI

As a boy I knew little of Africa. I grew up in Oakland, California, in the 1960s and 1970s and spent my childhood in the projects just down the street from the headquarters of the Black Panthers. Not only did I see the Panthers march and clash with the police, but I also ate in the local breakfast programs that the Panthers sponsored and colored in coloring books that they produced. This experience gave me an interest in the social and political events of the world. The books that I read in high school had no information about Africa, and little attention was paid to world events in my classes. One of my English teachers had us read a book on Frederick Douglass, Booker T. Washington, and W. E. B. Du Bois. This book inspired me to think in a broader fashion than before.

Then a series of events changed my life: I entered college and often heard Africa and the world mentioned; I learned about the antiapartheid movement and the struggle in Zimbabwe (at the time Rhodesia) and became actively involved in the divestment movement; I began to visit Africa on a regular basis. It was at college that I picked up the book *The Negro*, the first serious effort by W. E. B. Du Bois, the great Pan-African scholar, to write a continental history.

Tukufu Zuberi is the Lasry Family Professor of Race Relations and chair of the Department of Sociology at the University of Pennsylvania. He is a prominent scholar of African and African-American studies and race relations. Professor Zuberi joined the Penn faculty in 1989; during this time he has been a visiting professor at Makerere University in Uganda and at the University of Dar es Salaam in Tanzania. He holds a PhD from the University of Chicago. His publications include Swing Low, Sweet Chariot: The Mortality Cost of Colonizing Liberia in the Nineteenth Century *(University of Chicago Press 1995) and* Thicker than Blood: How Racial Statistics Lie *(University of Minnesota Press 2001). He is also the coeditor of* The Demography of South Africa *(M. E. Sharpe 2005) and* White Logic, White Methods *(Rowman & Littlefield 2008). The latter was the winner of the Oliver Cromwell Cox Book Award in 2009.*

DOI: 10.1177/0002716210378835

Fifty years ago, Martin Luther King Jr. found inspiration for his civil rights activities in the African independence movement; he even attended the 1957 celebration of independence in Accra, Ghana. Malcolm X spoke of the African independence movement as an example of a people's initiative in the face of great odds. In the spirit of W. E. B. Du Bois, these leaders of the civil rights and Black Power movements saw Africa as a guiding light.

As an academic, I have dedicated my career to writing about and studying Africa. Colonialism devastated most of Africa, and today parts of Africa are war-torn, yet much of the continent shows great promise and potential. It is for this latter reason that the world's attention is turning again toward this forgotten continent. As welcome as this new awareness is, the solutions to African problems are coming from Africans.

Perspectives on Africa and the World is a unique opportunity to provide fresh insight into the continent's past, present, and future by examining crucial historical turning points in African history over the past 75 years. In 2009, President Barack Obama said, "The twenty-first century will be shaped by what happens not just in Rome or Moscow or Washington, but by what happens in Accra as well" (Office of the Press Secretary 2009). Although Africa seems to most people to be a remote and impoverished place remembered for the suffering of its people, it has played an important role in recent history, and it will play a significant role in the future of America and the West in general.

American-led humanitarian intervention has often been based on ignorance, as in the lack of understanding why two U.S. military Black Hawk helicopters were shot down during the October 3–4, 1993, battle between Somalia militia forces and the U.S. military. This ignorance was also shown in our response to the genocides in Rwanda and, more recently, in the Sudan. This ignorance was also shown in our response to the genocides in Rwanda and, more recently, in the Sudan. The problem with considering Africa as a far-off land of which the American people know little is that the world has flattened politically, and America cannot afford to be ignorant of African realities. Ignoring Somalia because of its past failures leads to ship hijackings. Ignoring Nigeria makes it difficult for the average American to understand why a young terrorist from Nigeria would attempt to blow up a plane during a flight from Amsterdam to Detroit. Not paying attention to the Sudan has resulted in China's challenging America as the sole superpower. Understanding the reality of Africa in the 21st century requires viewing the continent within a broader context of recent world history. Through the lens of four watershed events—World War II, the end of colonialism, the cold war, and the new global interconnections—we can begin to see how Africa is shaped as much by what happens in America, Europe, Russia, and China as it is by events within its own borders. These events also reveal how much the rest of the world is shaped by events in Africa.

The world has long had contact with what we know today as Africa. The Greeks knew Africans as the "Libyes" (Libyans) of the north and the "Aithiops" (Ethiopians) of the south. The Romans later referred to the continent as "Afri." Thus, Africa, "the land of the Afri," originally referred to the Roman province established after the Roman conquest of Carthage in 146 BC. Following the fall of Rome and the rise of Arabic and Islam in the seventh century AD, the northern parts of the continent become known as "Ifriqiya" to the world. In the 15th century (the "age of discovery"), with the Portuguese voyages, the term "Africa" was applied to the entire continent. The Portuguese opened the gates of Africa to European merchants and politicians in a new way, which entailed a new way of thinking about Africa. This new way of thinking initiated a process that transformed both Africa and the world.

The context in which this change of thought and action occurred was the European enslavement of Africans. The point to understand here is that the modern idea of Africa emerged, in many ways, from the dehumanizing crucibles that were the European and Arabic systems of slavery. Meanwhile, in Europe and the United States, ideas about freedom and liberty were finding a new voice in the French and American Revolutions. Although ideas of democracy were taking root in Europe and the United States, both countries' political spheres required a justification for the mistreatment of Africa and Africans. And this is what led the greatest of European philosophers, Georg Hegel, to write in the 1830s that "what we properly understand by Africa, is the Unhistorical, Undeveloped Spirit, still involved in the conditions of mere nature, and which had to be presented here only as on the threshold of the World's History" (1956, 99).

The age of imperialism occurred during the late 19th and earlier 20th centuries. During this era, Western European nations, especially France and Britain, pursued aggressive policies to extend their political and economic control around the world. Joseph Chamberlain coined the term "new imperialism" in the 1890s in his capacity as the British colonial secretary who championed the British expansionist policies. The term was integrated into other European languages between 1880 and 1914. The British economist J. A. Hobson's *Imperialism*, written in 1902, and Vladimir Lenin's *Imperialism as the Highest Stage of Capitalism*, written in 1917, are key examples of critiques from the left. Yet the West maintained that imperialism was the only way to spread civilization in the world's underdeveloped areas.

The second largest continent, Africa is the cradle of mankind and home to some of the world's most ancient civilizations. Nearly 900 million people live in Africa, speaking some 900 languages and dialects and living in 53 different countries. Africa is so vast that you could put the landmasses of China, India, Argentina, New Zealand, and the continental United States within it and *still* not fill the entire continent. Africa stretches about 5,000 miles from Cape Blanc in Tunisia to Cape Agulhas in South Africa and is divided into Southern, East, Central, West, and North Africa. While Africa is geographically one continent, politically, culturally, economically, and socially, it is more diverse than are Europe, Asia, or the Americas. There is no one "Africa." The African continent has no unity of development, historical experience, physical characteristics, or religious identity. Not surprisingly, its history is varied and complex. The authors in this volume focus on the four watershed events mentioned above that changed the course of African and world history.

World War II was a global turning point and provided a deathblow to colonialism in Africa. An article in this volume documents the decisive role played by African soldiers in the Allied victory. Just as African-American soldiers fighting overseas returned from saving democracy in Europe to fight for civil rights at home, so African soldiers who had been fighting for their colonial masters went back to Africa demanding control over their own destinies. Future leaders of African countries and the African diaspora in Europe and the Americas met in 1945 in Manchester, England, at the fifth Pan-African Congress to consider next steps. These meetings were a catalyst for the independence movements spreading like forest fires across the continent.

Articles in this volume examine the degree to which these movements were about decolonization or national liberation. Both the United States and Russia demanded that France and Britain decolonize after World War II. Kwame Nkrumah, who organized the 1945 Pan-African Congress, became a symbol of African independence and led Ghana to independence from Britain in 1957. From Ghana, African and global forces came together in support of African independence to such an extent that the United Nations (UN) declared 1960 "The Year of Africa." More than 23 nations from Africa had joined the UN by that year. As the drive for freedom and self-rule accelerated, Africa seemed ready to enter a golden age where everything was possible. But after a few years, these nascent movements faltered as the cold war turned the dream of African independence into a nightmare.

Although World War II had ended, the cold war was writing its epilogue worldwide. Perhaps the greatest tragedy in post-colonial Africa was how the proxy conflict of the United States and the Soviet Union divided the continent along lines of global loyalty; newly independent African states were forced to take sides. In Africa, the cold war was fought with guns and bombs; gunfire was heard from South Africa to Nigeria, from the Congo to Algeria. It brought to power a new breed of leader who received international support only as long as he did what the United States or the Soviet Union wanted, not necessarily what was best for his people or nation. In South Africa, that meant support for the new system of apartheid; in Nigeria, this meant coup after coup after coup; and in the Congo, that meant Mobutu Sese Seko. The cold war in Africa meant the collapse of democratic hopes and possibilities. Across the continent, independence and democracy suffered.

America's ignorance of Africa's historical record has led to a tragic failure in assessing the causes of turmoil on the continent. Seeing Africa through shallow and misleading lenses of poverty, disease, and violence, coupled with the habit of ignoring the acts and social movements of the people of Africa, causes Africa's current problems and will continue to cause trouble for Africa until America and the rest of the "first world" come to terms with Africa's geopolitical importance. While I do not want to exaggerate the role of African history in world development, Africa has had a critical role.

On his 2009 trip to Africa, President Obama told the Ghanaian people, "This is the simple truth of a time when boundaries between people are overwhelmed by our connections. Your prosperity can expand America's prosperity. Your health and security can contribute to the world's health and security. And the strength of your democracy can help advance human rights for people everywhere. So, we do not see the countries and peoples of Africa as a world apart; we see Africa as a fundamental part of our interconnected world—as partners with America on behalf of the future we want for all of our children" (Office of the Press Secretary 2009).

The articles in this volume highlight the president's words by revealing the level of interconnection between African and world history. When Africa is relegated to the sidelines of world history, we all suffer the consequences. Much of what happens on the African continent has its origins in Washington, London, Paris, Moscow, or Beijing, just as events in Africa can shape the politics and economies of the world.

Perspectives on Africa and the World confronts how Africa arrived at its current situation. It can be argued that Africa entered World War II before Europe even recognized that such a war was being fought. On October 3, 1935, Benito Mussolini's fascist troops marched into Ethiopia, one of the two areas in Africa not under European colonialism. Four years later, Europe entered World War II with Hitler's invasion of Poland. During World War II, European nations and peoples who fell under Nazi rule were either put to work for the Reich or selected for extermination and destruction. From Africa's viewpoint, this was a case of the chickens coming home to roost in Europe. In Africa, European states habitually indentured and enslaved Asian and African populations for their own industrial and governmental benefits. Portugal, France, Britain, and other smaller colonizers used torture, mutilation, and mass murder to coerce the populace into obedience. Before World War Two, these brutal practices were unknown among Europeans west of the Bug and Prut Rivers.

Following the war, African political movements of the 1950s and 1960s succeeded in voicing a Pan-Africanist agenda. However, this legacy of unity, democracy, and progress was lost in the nightmare of political corruption of the 1970s and 1980s. The cold war and political corruption stole sovereignty from the people and placed it in the hands of tyrants such as Mobutu Sese Seko of Zaire. During the cold war, the concept of democracy was defined in terms of anticommunism. In most of Africa, democracy had little to do with the nature of government. Any African leader who stood against what was called communist totalitarianism could claim democracy regardless of how free the people in his regime really were. Interestingly, on the other side of the cold war, socialist states also claimed to be democratic, and African nation-states opposed to capitalist oppression were likewise considered democratic republics.

Most of the authors in this volume discuss whether aid, trade, and resistance to terror will remain as the pillars of Africa's future development. In recent years, while people outside of Africa sing "We Are the World" and organize "Band Aid," "Live Aid," and "Live 8," politicians demand more responsible aid with the Millennium Development Goals. While assistance from the world is crucial to Africa's future, African efforts to change the face of the continent's economy and forms of governance, and Africa's changing relationship with world security, are connected to Africa's obtaining its rightful place in the modern world.

During the post–cold war period, the idea of democracy in Africa has been separated from its cold war attachments. In the 1990s, a new symbol of democracy was born. Nelson Mandela and F. W. de Klerk received the Nobel Peace Prize in 1993. These two men in South Africa would come to symbolize democracy more than any others on the continent. De Klerk and Mandela represented two different sides of the struggle for African rights and political independence. De Klerk represented the party that introduced apartheid. Mandela was the international symbol of the fight against apartheid. This system of racial segregation was the longest-lasting symbol of colonial domination in Africa. De Klerk won the Nobel Prize because it was his reforms that led to the end of apartheid. Mandela won it because it was his struggle, strength, and integrity that led to the end of apartheid.

On April 24, 1994, the people of Pretoria, South Africa, awoke to the chants heard 50 years before in Manchester, England. Unlike the people of the nearly 50 nations who were liberated during the Pan-African Independence Movement, Africans in South Africa remained under the dominion of their colonial settlers until the end of the 20th century, when the Afrikaner-controlled National Party finally agreed to hold South Africa's first free, democratic elections. On April 24, 1994, the muted voices of millions of black South Africans were finally heard when they elected Nelson Mandela and his African National Congress (ANC) into power.

In some ways, South Africa's democracy is currently being challenged by the "split" of the ruling ANC, the rise of the leadership of Jacob Zuma, and the fall of former president Thabo Mbeki. However, a close examination suggests that these changes in leadership are the natural course of democracy in South Africa. Such changes represent a new image of democracy that has gripped the continent, and South Africa symbolizes this shift.

Democracy is important; however, alone it will not feed the people or provide health care. Good governance requires money. At the end of World War II, Africans stood with the Allies for the victory against fascism. As a result, Western Europe received aid and trade in the form of the Marshall Plan. This was a time when the United States was serious about development. Africa received independence, and this independence offered great hope. However, Africa received no Marshall Plans, and when aid did arrive, it came as a barrier to development. Things can be different for Africa in the 21st century. For things to be different, the world and Africa must change. That South Africa was the home of the 2010 Fifa World Cup is a clear indicator that Africa has arrived, and the world's most popular sport has played its most important games here. The issue is not whether Africa will play a role in the world's future; the conclusion is that Africa is central to the world's future.

The ideas in this volume were first presented at a conference I organized at the Center for Africana Studies at the University of Pennsylvania. The purpose of the conference was to present new research that examined social, political, and economic conditions in Africa from the World War II era through the periods of independence and the cold war, and leading up to present-day realities. The conference served as the basis for this special volume of *The Annals of the American Academy of Political and Social Science* on Africa. For decades, *The Annals* has been a leading voice in multidisciplinary scholarship, examining conditions on the African continent, with publications ranging from Thorsten Sellin's 1956 volume on *Africa and the Western World* to later volumes on *Africa in Motion* (1964), *Africa in Transition* (1977), and *International Affairs in Africa* (1987). It is our hope to continue this tradition in the 21st century with this volume on *Perspectives on Africa and the World*.

References

Hegel, Georg W. F. 1956. *The Philosophy of History*. Translated by J. Jibree. New York, NY: Dover.
Office of the Press Secretary. 11 July 2009. Remarks by the President to the Ghanaian Parliament. Accra, Ghana.

Black Africans in World War II: The Soldiers' Stories

JOHN H. MORROW Jr.

This article discusses the often forgotten contributions of black African infantry to the French and British war efforts from Europe to Asia during the Second World War. It traces the relationship between black African soldiers and their imperial rulers as it evolved over the course of two global conflicts from 1914 to 1945. The article points out how racist preconceptions about the "inferior" abilities and intelligence of Africans paralleled white Americans' prejudices against African-Americans and how the British and French attempted to systematically omit, diminish, or discredit the achievements of African soldiers.

Keywords: African infantry; askaris; King's African Rifles; Tirailleurs Sénégalais; Second World War

Essays on the topic of Africa in the Second World War, such as those in *Africa since 1935*, the eighth volume (1993) of the UNESCO *General History of Africa* edited by Ali A. Mazrui, devote precious little space to the experience of the African soldiers who fought on the various battlefields of the costliest and most extensive conflict in human history. Yet the subject of infantry such as the famed *Tirailleurs Sénégalais* of French West Africa and the King's African Rifles of British East Africa, who fought valiantly in both the First and the Second World Wars, merits sharper focus. These soldiers shed their blood for the right to equal treatment under their respective colonial regimes and, later, for the independence of their respective African nations from the colonial yoke.

Their struggle, in fact, paralleled that of the African-American soldiers who fought in both world wars to prove that black Americans merited the equality that white Americans denied

John H. Morrow Jr. is Franklin Professor of History at the University of Georgia. He specializes in the history of modern Europe and of warfare and society. His most recent book is The Great War: An Imperial History (Routledge 2004). He is currently working on a manuscript on the Second World War.

DOI: 10.1177/0002716210378831

ANNALS, AAPSS, 632, November 2010

them. Wartime service as combat soldiers and the willingness to fight and die for their country should have served as indisputable proof of their right to full and equal citizenship under the laws of the American republic. Instead, African-American claims met violent rejection, in the form of lynchings and race riots, at the hands of white Americans after World War I. After the Second World War, however, African-Americans, particularly soldiers, could tolerate discrimination no longer, and some white Americans recognized the injustice and waste in fielding segregated armed forces. President Harry Truman's desegregation of the armed forces in 1948, six years before the Supreme Court's decision in *Brown v. Topeka Board of Education*, signaled the federal government's intent to provide legal equality for black citizens. The relationship between black African soldiers and their imperial rulers evolved similarly over the course of two global conflicts from 1914 to 1945.

The Great War of 1914–1918, the most global war of its time, forced European empires to conscript colonial soldiers to meet their rising demands for manpower. Some 192,000 Senegalese *Tirailleurs*, conscripted from sub-Saharan Africa, fought on the Western Front and in Togo, Cameroon, and Turkey. The French particularly valued their *troupes indigènes* as assault troops on the Western Front. Some 30,000 to 31,000 West African soldiers lost their lives in the war, while many others suffered wounds or returned disabled from their service on these fronts (Mann 2006, 16–17). Had the war lasted into 1920, the French planned to deploy a million African infantrymen in the invasion of Germany. In the victory parade in November 1919 in Paris, Senegalese infantry enjoyed a prominent place among the ranks of the victorious French army. On the other hand, the army was concerned that many Senegalese soldiers who spent time in French hospitals developed a "warped mentality" because "spoiled by the nurses, admired by the people . . . they expect to be treated like Europeans" (Mann 2006, 166). The army thus attempted to "reSenegalize" the men using an amalgam of created cultural rituals to prepare the soldiers for their imminent return to Africa.

The British, on the other hand, refused to use "aboriginal" (African) troops in Europe, and only in 1916 did the British Empire raise West African units and send them and West Indian soldiers to East Africa, where German Colonel (later General) Paul von Lettow-Vorbeck's vaunted African *askaris*, warriors or infantry, were besting British, white South African, and Indian soldiers in a prolonged guerrilla war. In the Second World War, the descendants of the *askaris*, now subjects of the British Empire, served in the British imperial forces as soldiers of the King's African Rifles side by side with their West African counterparts.

The French African *Tirailleurs*

After World War I, the French occupation forces in Germany included two regiments of West African soldiers, whom the French government had sent to the Rhineland in order to demobilize French soldiers and to "reward" the Africans for services rendered to the French nation during four years of war.

French government officials, such as Premier Georges Clemenceau and Blaise Diagne, the Senegalese deputy who had played the key role in recruiting Senegalese soldiers in return for benefits and more equal rights, also hoped to impress upon their African soldiers/subjects the power of a victorious France. Then they would return to "the various regions of our West African colonies; the turbulent populations impressed by the power of France [would] no longer be tempted to cause disturbances" (Fogarty 2008, 280).

Although the historical records show that the black African soldiers behaved well toward their German charges, the German government and propagandists portrayed them as "savages" guilty of every crime imaginable. The resulting hue and cry about "*Die Schwarze Schande*" or "*Smach*," the "Black Shame" in the Rhineland, played upon the racist attitudes of British and American reporters, who took up the call of "the black horror on the Rhine" (see Scheck 2006, 98–101). The French removed the West African troops in June 1920.

In the process of repatriating the West African soldiers, the French government reneged on its wartime promises of January 1918 to grant the veterans pensions and the same rights as French citizens and naturalization if they so desired. "Republican tradition and history created a close link between service to the state in the military and the rights and duties of citizens," observed historian Richard Fogarty, "but efforts to offer naturalization to soldiers, thus bringing their service into line with republican principles, foundered upon allegedly insurmountable racial and cultural difference" (Fogarty 2008, 273). As a consequence, West African veterans justifiably concluded that the governments in Paris and Dakar, Senegal, had mistreated and abandoned them by failing to enforce such wartime promises.

In a few cases, World War I veterans remained in the army and attained ranks as commissioned officers. Captain Charles N'Tchóréré, a native of Gabon, served in the last years of the war and rose to become commander of the academy for military cadets in St. Louis, Senegal, before retiring after 20 years of service. In the interwar years, the French army continued its conscription of West African recruits, and a total of some 250,000 served during the interwar years, with 48,000 in the ranks annually (Mann 2006, 85). The French army regularly posted them to garrisons in southern France.

When war broke out in Europe, from 1939 to June 1940, the French army summoned some 300,000 North African and 197,000 West African men to the colors. On the eve of the German invasion of France, an estimated 75,000 Senegalese infantry were in Métropole France. In May 1940, seven African divisions and three mixed colonial divisions in a French army of 80 divisions awaited the German onslaught. Some 63,300 West Africans saw combat in France in 1940 in eight colonial regiments (RTS—*Régiment de Tirailleurs Sénégalais*) and eight mixed regiments of colonial and metropolitan infantry (RICMS—*Régiment d'infanterie coloniale mixte sénégalais*). Among them Capt. Charles N'Tchóréré, who had reactivated his commission, commanded a company of the 53rd Regiment on the Somme not far from where his son, Corporal Jean-Baptiste, was deployed (Echenberg 1985, 368; Scheck 2006, 17).

The 1st and 6th Colonial Divisions on the Aisne River and in the Argonne bore the brunt of the German panzer invasion in May 1940, while the 4th and 5th Colonial Divisions bore the brunt of the German attacks on the Somme River after May 22. The African soldiers fought tenaciously and retreated in good order. However, many black Africans believed that French units "succumbed to demoralization and defeatism," leaving them to cover the retreat of French soldiers and to suffer heavy casualties in their determined resistance to the Germans (Echenberg 1985, 368). In battles on the Somme in early June, the French resorted to "hedgehog" tactics, letting superior German units pass and then attacking them from the rear, while the Africans engaged the Germans in bitter close combat and house-to-house fighting. In response, Gen. Erwin Rommel's 7th Panzer Division conducted "cleansing operations" against dispersed Senegalese and summarily executed captured soldiers (Scheck 2006, 24–26).

Gen. Hans Hube, commander of the German 16th Infantry Division, strenuously objected to France's use of West African troops, which he deemed "a shame and dishonor, all the more so because our division has had to wage the hardest fights against the Negroes" (Scheck 2006, 69). German soldiers, stoked on Nazi propaganda that declared the West Africans to be illegitimate combatants, "bestial, savage, and perfidious," and thoroughly shocked and enraged at the casualties they suffered against the Africans' staunch resistance, massacred some 3,000 West African wounded soldiers and prisoners of war (POWs) in the western campaign (Scheck 2006, 9, 58).

Capt. N'Tchérér's *Tirailleurs* fought off several German attacks on June 5 and 6, 1940, at the village of Airaines. When the Germans finally captured the village and the African soldiers on June 7, a young Panzer officer insisted that the black captain line up with his enlisted men, not the captured French officers. When Capt. N'Tchérér protested, the German shot him in the neck. His son, Jean-Baptiste, fell in combat the same day. Later, German soldiers massacred 50 of Capt. N'Tchérér's African soldiers and virtually annihilated the 53rd Regiment, which suffered nearly 90 percent casualties. At the armistice, some 10,000 West Africans had been killed, and half of the nearly 15,000 West African POWs would not survive German POW camps (Scheck 2006, 27–28). Historian Raffael Scheck discerns the elements of a "race war" in the campaign in the West and concludes that "the German Wehrmacht did conduct a race war against black Africans in the Western campaign of 1940" and that "they dealt with the black soldiers in a way that anticipated the horrors of the racialized warfare associated with the later German campaigns in the Balkans and the Soviet Union" (Scheck 2006, 3).

Two sons of Félix Eboué, the Guyanese governor of Chad who was the first high-ranking official in French Africa to side with de Gaulle's Free French and who would later become governor-general of French Equatorial Africa, became POWs (Lawler 1992, 122). One POW, Léopold Sédar Senghor, was released on medical grounds in 1942 to resume his career as a teacher at a *lycée* in the Parisian suburb of Joinville. Born in Senegal in 1906, the son of a merchant who raised his son Catholic, Senghor was educated in French schools, completed his education at the Sorbonne, and became the first African to pass the *aggrégation*—examinations that entitled one to teach in a French *lycée*. He became a French citizen in 1934—an *évolué*—literally, one who had "evolved." Senghor would further espouse the concept of Négritude and the ideology of Pan-Africanism, because the alienation he had experienced in France forced him and others similar to him to confront "their authentic selves." After serving in the Resistance during the Second World War, he returned to Africa as part of a mass repatriation of *évolués* who had remained in France during the 1920s and 1930s (Scheck 2006, 49, 58; Echenberg 1985, 372; Genova 2004, 117, 137, 150, 168, 191, 205).

During the German occupation of France, the Vichy government repatriated most Senegalese soldiers to West Africa, where they became a forgotten generation. Vichy did send some 16,000 Senegalese infantrymen to North Africa and some 4,000 to the Middle East. When Allied units entered Syria and Lebanon in June 1941, Vichyite Senegalese fought Senegalese infantry serving in the Free French forces. After the Vichy defeat, most of the Vichyite *Tirailleurs* in the Levant joined the Free French rather than be repatriated to West Africa, and 1,500 of them became part of the famous Free French First Division. Free French generals expressed concerns about the reliability of their former enemies, as the Africans "[were] armed and trained to the teeth. Paternalism [was] no more. [They had] created gladiators with a powerful armament" (Lawler 1992, 152–53). Their concerns were baseless. The Senegalese soldiers suppressed a revolt in Syria in May 1942, while 1,000 had arrived in Egypt in December 1941 to fight in North Africa with the British Eighth Army against Rommel's Afrika Korps. They fought at Bir Hakeim, where the French sacrificed themselves to delay Rommel's attack, and later, when there were more than 2,000 infantry, at Alamein and across North Africa in the British advance in October and November 1942 (Lawler 1992, 154–57).

French West African soldiers participated in the invasions of Sicily and Italy and fought in the Italian theater of war. Twelve thousand of them liberated the island of Elba, the birthplace of Napoleon, in June 1944. Twenty thousand West African infantry participated in the invasion of southern France and fought in the campaign moving north through southern France, ultimately liberating the city of Belfort in eastern France in November 1944. Yet this was their last victory, because the West African soldiers in Gen. Jean de Lattre de Tassigny's First French army were then summarily relieved of their uniforms and weapons without warning starting in September and October, grouped with the remaining African POWs liberated from German *Stalags*, and sent to the south of France for repatriation to West Africa (Echenberg 1985, 373–74).

These black African soldiers had fallen victim to the policy of *Blanchissement*. Gen. Charles de Gaulle had a politically expedient policy of "whitening" the French army by replacing them with French conscripts and partisans to exaggerate the importance of the French Resistance. De Gaulle sought to emphasize the French role in the liberation, to control the Resistance and particularly the communists in it, and to restore French self-confidence—at the expense and humiliation of Senegalese *Tirailleurs* who had fought loyally and valiantly for France for four years (Echenberg 1985, 375–76).

In London in January 1944, de Gaulle had insisted that his Frenchmen lead the liberation of Paris. In return, British and American generals, specifically British Gen. Frederick Morgan and Eisenhower's chief of staff, Maj. Gen. Walter Bedell Smith, informed de Gaulle that the division should "consist of white personnel." Smith further suggested that "the French 2nd Armored Division . . . with only one fourth native personnel, [was] the only French division operationally available that could be made one hundred percent white" (Thomson 2009).

All other French units, specifically infantry divisions, were only 40 percent white and 60 percent North and West African soldiers. The French 2nd Armored Division did lead the liberation of Paris in August 1944, but many of its personnel were Spanish refugees from Francisco Franco's authoritarian regime. To "whiten" the other French divisions, the French used soldiers from North Africa and the Middle East. From 1943 to 1945, 385,000 men from North Africa, including 290,000 Algerians, Tunisians, and Moroccans, fought in the liberation of Corsica, in the campaigns in Italy and southern France, and joined the main French army for the rest of the war.

After this humiliating summary dismissal, the West Africans languished in camps in the south of France until late November 1944 for lack of transport. After some 15 bloody clashes had occurred in France, the worst violence happened in Senegal in the Thiaroye transit camp outside Dakar on December 1, 1944. One thousand two hundred and eighty ex-POWs rioted because they had received no back pay or demobilization premiums; their guards opened fire on them, killing 35, seriously wounding another 30, and injuring hundreds more. This notorious incident, immortalized in fiction and film, left returning French West African veterans with a sense of a "shared experience" of struggle and the French government's ingratitude for their service. This sense of a collective group endured in West African veterans' associations, which played an important part in the struggle during the 1940s for pensions, benefits, and, ultimately, equality before the law (Echenberg 1985, 376–79).

Historian Martin Thomas concluded that in concentrating on metropolitan France, de Gaulle's provisional government made a "grave error in failing to highlight the pivotal contribution of colonial troops to the Free French military effort between 1940 and 1944" (Thomas 1998, 253). In contrast to the Africans' place of prominence in the French victory parade of 1919, the French government paid "limited official recognition of their achievements during the victory celebrations of 1945." The severity, in general, of the French treatment of their black African troops and, in particular, of the French response to the unrest among the *Tirailleurs*, "bore witness to the failure of French political memory regarding its colonial soldiers" and suggested that the "Gaullist emphasis upon France's debt to its empire was empty rhetoric." The French Empire "never entirely recovered from the rifts that had opened up between rulers and ruled" during the Second World War (Thomas 1998, 263).

Although West African veterans remained among the most consistent supporters of the French presence in Africa in order for the French government to fulfill its obligations to them, one group started the first independence movement in

West Africa after the war, the *Mouvement Nationaliste Africain* (Chafer 2002, 46–7). Senegalese war veterans particularly appreciated the candidacy of one of their own, Léopold Senghor, who wore khaki and sunglasses during his campaign in rural Senegal for election to the French Constituent Assembly in October 1945. Perhaps the most poignant symbol of France's failure to own up to the debt it owed the *Tirailleurs Sénégalais* was that after the war in Bamako, Mali, Ma Diarra, the widow of the heroic Capt. Charles N'Tchoréré, could not obtain the pension owed to her (Mann 2006, 128).

The British West African Frontier Force and King's African Rifles of East Africa

For British African forces, and for Africa in general and Ethiopia in particular, the Second World War started in 1935, when Italian Fascist dictator Benito Mussolini's European and colonial forces invaded and conquered Ethiopia with the intention of reversing the humiliating defeat that Italian forces had suffered at the hands of the Ethiopians at Adowa in 1896. The conquest proved an extremely brutal affair, as Mussolini's troops, emulating French, Italian, and Spanish colonial forces that had fought brutal wars to suppress rebellions in North Africa during the 1920s, employed the most highly toxic gases developed during the First World War against the Ethiopians. Although the Italian imperial forces conquered Ethiopia, they did not succeed in crushing internal opposition to their rule despite resorting to the most brutal methods, from massacres to deportation.

The Italian conquest galvanized resentment against European rule in Africa and Pan-Africanist sentiment among East and West African elites and future leaders such as Nnamdi Azikiwe of Nigeria, Jomo Kenyatta of Kenya, Kwame Nkrumah of Ghana, and I. T. A. Wallace-Johnson of Sierra Leone (Sbacchi 1985, 233–35). Mussolini, of course, paid no attention and was more intent, once his ally Adolf Hitler unleashed war on the European continent in 1939, on increasing still further his African empire. In 1940 he consequently unleashed attacks from his empire in the Horn of Africa against neighboring British colonies. The British responded by mobilizing white South African troops and black African soldiers from the West African Frontier Force and from the King's African Rifles in East Africa—the latter were the descendants of the *askaris* from the former German East African colonies—to thwart the Italians. In the East African campaign against Mussolini, the Nigerian Brigade staged a long and rapid advance into Ethiopia, only to be held outside the capital, Addis Ababa, to allow the white South African troops to enter the capital city first (Hamilton 2001, 340).

After the transfer of Ethiopia from Italy (a colony of) to Britain (a protectorate of), the soldiers of the West African Frontier Force formed the 81st and 82nd (West African) Divisions, and the soldiers of the King's African Rifles formed the 11th (East Africa) Division. At the suggestion of Sir George Giffard, inspector general of African forces, in December 1942, the three divisions were destined for service in the 14th Army of British Imperial Forces fighting against the Japanese in Burma, in the China-Burma-India theater of war (Hamilton 2001, 35). The British continued to adhere to their policy from the war of 1914–1918 of deploying only African labor battalions and no "aboriginal" combat troops in Europe.

All four of Britain's West African colonies—The Gambia, the Gold Coast, Nigeria, and Sierra Leone—provided units in the Frontier Force and consequently the West African divisions. British colonial authorities even recruited from tribes such as the Ashanti in the Gold Coast and the Yoruba in southwest Nigeria that they had normally avoided before the war, because they regarded the higher-educated indigenous peoples as potential troublemakers. Throughout the British Empire—and West and East Africa offered no exception—the British definition of "martial" tribesmen, their ideal recruits, coincided with the uneducated and less educated. The prewar Nigerian and Gold Coast Regiments used Hausa as their common language as they recruited primarily from uneducated tribes, but with the expansion of recruitment to include more educated tribes, the common language became pidgin English, a fortunate change as a number of the division's new officers were Polish officers who had survived and fled the German invasion of their homeland. Hamilton also averred that in the absence of white settlers in West Africa, an attempt to send white Rhodesians as officers failed, as their attitudes toward "bloody Kaffirs" were "not helpful" (Hamilton 2001, 26, 32–33).

Some 23,000 West African "volunteers," actually conscripts, 3,000 of whom were infantry, sailed in troopships around the Horn of Africa and into the Indian Ocean, destined for service in some of the most forbidding climates and terrain in any theater of the conflict. They formed the 81st Division for first-line combat, which included 28 battalions unique for their dependence on carriers or porters. The 81st was the largest concentration of African troops ever assembled, much larger than any unit that the British mobilized between 1914 and 1918, and it included artillery and antiaircraft units and a medical corps. Its reliance on human transport, so reminiscent of the First World War, appeared at first glance an anachronism ill suited for a war of machines that relied on automotive or aerial transport. Ironically, these very porters or carriers prepared the West Africans to fight in the northwest extremity of Burma, the north Arakan. Brigadier Swynnerton of the 1st (West African) Brigade observed that his men were the only soldiers in Burma who were "capable of operating for months on end in the worst country in the world, without vehicles and without mules, and [were] alone able to carry all [their] warlike stores with [them]" (Hamilton 2001, 28). The infantrymen wore standard jungle green British fatigues; carried the standard Enfield rifle with bayonet, "Mills bombs," rifle grenades, and a Bren or light machine gun for each infantry section; and were supported by light artillery. Japanese infantry had heavier weapons, medium machine guns, and even 37-millimeter, high-velocity antitank cannons for use against infantry. The African carriers, in practice designated "unarmed soldiers," wore the same equipment as infantry and were actually trained to use infantry weapons. They cleared drop zones, collected supplies dropped from the air, and cleared airstrips for the evacuation of wounded soldiers. But they could also defend themselves, and as the campaign continued, 40 percent of the carriers were armed with the lightweight automatic Sten gun and a few Bren guns.

The Arakan's narrow jungle valleys, cut by *chaungs* (streams or rivers) and ending in mangrove swamps, were bounded on both sides by steep hills covered thickly with bamboo stalks 18 feet high and topped by narrow ridges. From these steep hills rose high mountains. The valleys, ridges, and mountains were negotiable only by narrow paths impassable to animal and motor transport. The southwest monsoon regularly drenched the region with as much as 200 inches of rain between May and November. The days were hot and the nights cold and damp; diseases such as scrub typhus, malaria, and cholera abounded.

In January 1944, the men of the 81st Division headed into the dense jungle and hills on the northern flank of the imperial army to drive the Japanese southeast out of Burma. Imbued with an offensive attitude, the West Africans moved at a rate of some eight miles per day through the bush. The Africans remained in the jungle for six months, receiving supplies by air for five of them—some three months longer than Orde Wingate's famed Chindits survived behind Japanese lines. The Africans covered more ground than any Chindit column, as they moved rapidly over mountainous jungle where no roads or pack animals could penetrate (Hamilton 2001, 159).

The voices of the West and East African soldiers are not available, but British authors who served as junior officers with them during the campaign have rescued their soldiers from obscurity within the past decade. John A. L. Hamilton, a company intelligence officer in the 81st, was particularly galled by 14th Army commander Gen. William Slim's statement that the African soldiers would be "lost" if left on their own without British junior officers. Hamilton consequently liberally sprinkled his narrative with accounts of derring-do on the part of African noncommissioned officers and enlisted men and platoons led by African noncoms that demonstrated their bravery, initiative, and sound tactical sense. In the process, the African soldiers were awarded the Military Medal and the Distinguished Conduct Medal for heroism and gallantry, but the British Empire's highest medal, the Victoria Cross, was denied to Africans.

In an encounter where the Japanese forces suffered severe casualties in overrunning an Indian artillery unit attached to the African soldiers, the Sikh officer in command of the guns received the Victoria Cross. British officers penned a doggerel that went in part, "The next day Corps replied, a VC you must pick,/Say a dead Gurkha or part-damaged Sikh/For the Africans, voteless, are not worth a damn—/You might just as well decorate Kaladan Sam [a nickname for the Japanese soldier]" (Hamilton 2001, 227).

That Africans were deliberately denied the Victoria Cross is analogous to the African-American experience in the First and Second World Wars, as the U.S. Army refused to award the Congressional Medal of Honor to any African-American soldier. Only during the Clinton administration did the Army award a limited number long after the events and after a number of the former soldiers had died of natural causes.

As Hamilton's account above makes eminently clear, the African soldiers proved to be highly capable troops in the difficult conditions of Burma. Hamilton was particularly impressed with the African NCOs (noncommissioned officers), whose illiteracy necessitated that they literally memorize the weapon training manual and who "managed well without a white man to guide" them (Hamilton 2001, 115). He cited engagements in which "Africans controlled their fire admirably and coolly, relying mainly on grenades, their favourite weapon, which was the preferred close-quarters weapon in jungle war, not the bayonet" (Hamilton 2001, 149).

This last observation about preference for the grenade stands in sharp contrast to French African soldiers, whose white commanders in both world wars often not only preferred but ordered them to use their long knives, or *coupe-coupes*, whenever possible, to strike fear into the hearts of their German enemy as they rushed forward to engage in fighting at close quarters. The African soldiers expressed their preference for pistols, because the Germans took advantage of their lack of firearms to shoot them in the back in hand-to-hand combat. The Senegalese infantry would have much preferred to kill the Germans straight out rather than merely strike fear in their hearts. In the campaign of 1940, German troops occasionally massacred captured African troops using the Africans' long knives as retribution for their possession.

In contrast, the West Africans attacked with the Bren gun and grenades, charging straight up near-vertical ascents and 60 yards across open ground to attack Japanese bunkers, or executing wide-ranging flanking movements to strike the Japanese. They also attacked with fixed bayonets when necessary. These soldiers excelled not only in attack, but also in retreat. In prolonged encounters with Japanese, who outnumbered them, individual soldiers effectively covered their retreating patrols with enfilades, even when wounded. Nigerian Sergeant Dogo Yerwa, despite wounds from grenade splinters, led his platoon effectively, moving from section to section to ensure their selection of enemy targets, accuracy of fire, and conservation of ammunition, as the Africans repulsed a seven-hour attack by a company of Japanese soldiers (Hamilton 2001, 225).

The war in Burma was a struggle between smaller units of company, through platoon, down to squad—a subaltern (junior commissioned officer) and sergeant's war. The loss of commissioned officers meant that African sergeants and sergeant-majors led platoons and patrols. The 81st Division's officers included Lieutenant Seth Anthony, trained in England and the first African to hold the King's commission (Hamilton 2001, 46). All African units suffered substantial and irreplaceable losses among their European officers, but they continued to function because their African NCOs stepped up to the mark and led the men effectively. The 81st Division consequently advanced and captured Myohaung, the ancient capital of Arakan, so quickly that they enabled the main British imperial force to capture its objective of Akyab Island without fighting, because the Japanese had withdrawn for fear of being outflanked. Hamilton observed that the division's unique mobility in the jungle, which the men regarded as a friend that cloaked their movements to outmaneuver the Japanese, would have actually enabled the West Africans to advance even farther and faster had the army not restrained them to conform with advances on the main front. The army congratulated its commandos for their capture of Akyab but was silent about the Africans' capture of Myohaung (Hamilton 2001, 83, 243, 260).

The West Africans received very little notice from the 14th Army. The public relations officer (PRO) of the West African Expeditionary Force observed cynically that they "went in anonymously, marched out anonymously, and it seems they have left anonymous dead behind them. . . . [T]hey have remained anonymous . . . in all the written records of the Far East War." The PRO went on to write, "This campaign was the only one which no war correspondent covered." The 14th Army's commanders seldom visited the 81st Division, resulting in the division's being "out of sight and out of mind." Hamilton acerbically commented, "It seems that no one had noticed 20,000 men . . . operating in enemy territory all that time; perhaps black faces did not show up in the jungle" (Hamilton 2001, 21–22, 159, 163, 342). This unfortunate circumstance led to the failure of British historians of the war to give the 81st Division the credit that it merited and to ignore, or even to denigrate, the service of the African soldiers.

At least the West Africans did receive some accolades from their commanders, as the men's endurance, strength, stamina, and intelligence came to the attention of Division Commander Maj. Gen. Loftus Tottenham, a former commander of Gurkhas (Hamilton 2001, 197). Gen. Brian Leese's official dispatch also recognized their achievements. With no means of transport via land, limited communication or physical contact with the outside world, and slender resources, the 81st (West African) Division had beaten back parts of the Japanese 54th and 55th Divisions and cleared the greater part of the Kaladan Valley. "For the first time, divisions from East and West Africa [the 11th, 81st, and 82nd] were fighting as complete formations with the British Commonwealth Forces, and they had shown outstanding ability to endure terrible conditions of terrain and climate" (Hamilton 2001, 258). Perhaps most significant, the debriefing of Japanese commanders revealed that they considered both West and East African soldiers "the best jungle fighters" of the Allies for their ability to penetrate the flanks of Japanese positions and for rescuing their dead and wounded after an action (Nunneley 1998, 5; Hamilton 2001, 9).

When the army sent the 81st Division to the rear at the end of its deployment in Burma, it sent the soldiers to the heat of the Madras plains in India some hundred miles upcountry from the city of Madras. After nearly 18 months away from civilization, the disappointed soldiers languished in isolation from mid-March until December 1945, when they shipped out for home. The 81st Division returned to West Africa in December 1945 to be demobilized by March 1946, although a detachment did march in the Victory Parade in London in June 1946. In colonies such as the Gold Coast, part of the future state of Ghana, and Nigeria, returning soldiers could channel their aspirations through the political parties that were demanding self-government, and in 1948, veterans played a key role in Kwame Nkrumah's rise to power in Ghana.

In the King's African Rifles from East Africa, John Nunneley served as a British officer in the 6th Battalion (Tanganyika Territory), as British officers and senior NCOs were "seconded" or attached to African regiments for the duration of the conflict. "Colonial" officers, East African white planters, returned to their farms in a general imperial attempt to increase food production, and were replaced by "imperials" such as Nunneley who were sent out from Britain. His company's *askaris* came mostly from the Tanganyikan tribes such as the Nyamwezi, Wagogo, Chagga, Sukuma, a few Hehe, and a strong contingent of Yao from the south, but a few came from as far away as Sudan and the West Nile, and one all the way from the Gold Coast. According to Nunneley, few soldiers in the East African forces were Christian or Muslim; rather, most of them were pagans who celebrated in dance and feast to the beat of the *ngoma*, the drum (Nunneley 1998, 32–33, 62).

Nunneley cited the material benefits of military service, such as regular meals, as an attraction for men from impoverished areas, but he emphasized the "intangible but immense lifelong prestige" of being an *askari* of the King's African Rifles as the major lure. The African soldiers' fitness, strength, and "astonishing" endurance enabled them to apply the "intensely physical" new battle drill of infantry tactics, displaying coordinated and disciplined actions at the sound of the officer's whistle. They quickly mastered running, crawling, surmounting obstacles, attacking and charging with the bayonet, and deploying to form pincer movements in an attack (Nunneley 1998, 35–36).

The army's wartime need for specialists in signals and other trades prompted the recruitment of the Kikuyu for the first time because of their superior knowledge compared with the "martial" tribes such as the Kalenji and the Kamba, although the British deemed the Kikuyu "notorious troublemakers." This amalgam of various tribes, led by British officers such as Nunneley, sailed first for Ceylon. Nunneley had passed written and oral examinations in Swahili, which enabled him to communicate with his *askaris* and censor the mail that professional letter writers had drafted on behalf of soldiers or their families at home. In transit from Mombasa, Kenya, to Colombo, Ceylon, in early 1944, the transport *Khedive Ismail* fell victim to Japanese torpedoes in the Indian Ocean and there was heavy loss of life. Of the 1,511 passengers on board, 30 of 199 British officers and 113 of 787 *askaris* survived (Nunneley 1998, 84, 107, 117).

The East Africans, similar to their West African counterparts, proved superb soldiers, calm and confident, in Nunneley's judgment. Although most East African soldiers came from open spaces such as plains, hills, or desert, Nunneley concluded that their acute powers of observation made them especially good trackers and patrol leaders in jungle warfare. Under pressure from the 14th Army command, they advanced at high speed down the Kaladan Valley. In Nunneley's opinion, the pace resulted in insufficient reconnaissance and avoidable casualties, but the soldiers' morale remained high despite their casualties (Nunneley 1998, 151, 156, 167).

During their deployment to Ceylon and then Burma, Nunneley noted three incidents in which African NCOs and enlisted men of his company struck back after punishment for infractions of regulations. The King's African Rifles resorted to lashes with the *kiboko*, or rhino-hide whip, for major infractions. Cowardice in the face of the enemy merited the death penalty. Nunneley does not cite the punishment for the initial crimes committed by the African soldiers, but in retribution for them a sergeant shot and killed three officers before he was gunned down, and two enlisted men faced the firing squad, the first for shooting and killing an officer and the second for killing one officer and wounding five others with a grenade (Nunneley 1998, 65–67, 108, 172). If the initial punishment entailed 12 lashes—a standard number—in front of the unit, these soldiers may have resented this humiliation, which smacked of slavery, so greatly that they felt obliged to kill the officers who were responsible, even if it meant their certain death. Furthermore, these African soldiers clearly feared neither their white officers nor death, potentially an ominous portent for postwar relationships in British East Africa.

After the Second World War, two of the African NCOs in Nunneley's battalion rose to command, first in the ranks of the Mau Mau rebels in the late 1940s and early 1950s and later in Jomo Kenyatta's Kenyan army. Waruhiu Itote, one of a few Kikuyus in the battalion, became "General China" in the Mau Mau military command structure, and later Kenyatta appointed him second in command of the National Youth Service. Juma Ndolo, a Kamba, attended Officers Training Command in England after the war and ultimately rose to command the Kenyan army with the rank of major general before his retirement in the early 1970s (Nunneley 1998, 67–68).

Conclusion

The service of black African infantry in the ranks of French and British imperial forces has not received the attention it merits from historians, because contemporary European observers usually either ignored or denigrated their service. Racist preconceptions about the "inferior" abilities and intelligence of Africans paralleled white Americans' prejudices against African-Americans. These American combat soldiers disappeared from the history of the war, to receive only negative mention when white historians denigrated the achievements of black soldiers, whether African or American, as a race; although these historians never attributed to their race the similar performance on the part of European or white American soldiers.

Fortunately, in recent years, a few European officers who fought in African units have begun to rescue their comrades and units from obscurity. Correspondingly, a few young and talented scholarly historians such as Gregory Mann and Richard Fogarty have joined such predecessors as Myron Echenberg and Nancy Ellen Lawler to research the archives and to interview survivors to shed valuable light on the experiences and achievements of French black African soldiers in both world wars. Similar scholarly historical work remains to be done on British black African soldiers.

In the absence of much concrete research, historical debate has swirled around the number of veterans participating in postwar politics and independence movements. Yet the number is less important than the essential point that many of them did, and very effectively, and all desired to have perceived wrongs righted and to enjoy the legitimate benefits for their services. They had paid, in French terminology, the *impôt du sang*, or blood tax, and if not independence, they certainly sought equality. The British and French attempts to omit, diminish, or discredit the achievements of African soldiers stemmed from their intent to ignore or limit

African demands for equality and independence, in the same fashion that white Americans' refusal to acknowledge the combat service of African-American soldiers was intended to keep the latter "in their place" and forestall the granting of equal rights to black citizens under the law.

African combat soldiers of World War II, similar to their African-American counterparts, consequently became forgotten soldiers. In particular, soldiers from British East and West Africa fought in the 14th Army in the Burmese campaign in the China-Burma-India theater, often referred to by historians as the "Forgotten Army" in the "Forgotten War." The African soldiers epitomize the "forgotten soldiers" of that "forgotten" struggle, just as their French African and African-American counterparts became the "forgotten" soldiers of their armies. Historians are now in the process of rescuing these men from obscurity so that history might reflect their very real contributions to the allied war effort in the Second World War, the most momentous conflict in history.

References

Chafer, Tony. 2002. *The end of empire in French West Africa: France's successful decolonization?* New York, NY: Berg.

Echenberg, Myron. 1985. Morts pour la France; the African soldier in France during the Second World War. *Journal of African History* 26:363–80.

Fogarty, Richard S. 2008. *Race and war in France: Colonial subjects in the French army, 1914–1918.* Baltimore, MD: Johns Hopkins University Press.

Genova, James E. 2004. *Colonial ambivalence, cultural authenticity, and the limitations of mimicry in French-ruled West Africa.* New York, NY: Peter Lang.

Hamilton, John A. L. 2001. *War Bush. 81 (West African) division in Burma 1943–1945.* Norwich, UK: Michael Russell.

Lawler, Nancy Ellen. 1992. *Soldiers of misfortune. Ivoirien Tirailleurs of World War II.* Athens, OH: Miami University Press.

Mann, Gregory. 2006. *Native sons: West African veterans and France in the twentieth century.* Durham, NC: Duke University Press.

Nunneley, John. 1998. *Tales from the King's African Rifles: A last flourish of empire.* London, UK: Cassell.

Sbacchi, Alberto. 1985. *Ethiopia under Mussolini. Fascism and the colonial experience.* London, UK: Zed Books.

Scheck, Raffael. 2006. *Hitler's African victims: The German army massacres of Black French soldiers in 1940.* New York, NY: Cambridge University Press.

Thomas, Martin. 1998. *The French empire at war 1940–45.* Manchester, UK: Manchester University Press.

Thomson, Mike. 6 April 2009. Paris liberation made "Whites Only." BBC News Radio 4. Available from newsvote.bbc.co.uk.

The Ogaden War and the Demise of Détente

By
DONNA R. JACKSON

The failure of détente has been a popular theme among historians of American foreign policy, with opinions divided as to where the responsibility for this failure lies. A commonality among all points of view, however, is the importance of events in the third world, particularly in the "Arc of Crisis." One such event—the Ogaden War between Ethiopia and Somalia—prompted Zbigniew Brzezinski, President Carter's national security advisor, to comment that détente was "buried" in the Ogaden. His point was that Carter's new approach to the cold war was put to the test during the Ogaden War, and there the policy's untenability was proven. The policy's failure, in turn, encouraged Soviet adventurism, which further alienated the American public from Carter's attempt to fight the cold war. Carter's policy eventually led to the withdrawal of the SALT II (Strategic Arms Limitation Talks) Treaty and, as Brzezinski claimed, the collapse of détente. This article discusses Carter's foreign policy toward the Ogaden War, considers the accuracy of Brzezinski's claim, and reaches conclusions regarding the role of the Carter administration in the demise of détente.

Keywords: Carter; détente; Ethiopia; Somalia; Ogaden; Strategic Arms Limitation Talks (SALT)

In 1980, the Carter administration, which had been engaging in debates for two years over the direction and implementation of foreign policy, halted its equivocation. Jimmy Carter's reorientation, from a foreign policy that emphasized regionalism and human rights to one that emphasized more traditional cold war themes such as globalism and containment, seemed, to some historians, to signal the demise of détente and the onset of a second cold war.

The failure of détente has been a popular theme among historians of recent American

Donna R. Jackson is senior lecturer in modern history in the Department of History and Archaeology at the University of Chester, with particular specialties in American history and foreign policy. She was previously a research fellow at Wolfson College, Cambridge, UK.

DOI: 10.1177/0002716210378833

foreign policy. As with the beginning of the cold war in the 1940s, academic opinion is divided over the reasons for the hardening of relations in the late 1970s. Some historians argue that one of the superpowers was overly aggressive, thus betraying the spirit of détente. Fred Halliday, for example, claims that the American determination to rebuild its position of strength, damaged by the experience of Vietnam in particular, was ultimately responsible (Halliday 1986). An alternative perspective, as put forward by analysts including Raymond Garthoff, Jussi Hanhimaki, and Odd Arne Westad, divides the responsibility between both superpowers. In general, this historiographical viewpoint argues that both the United States and the Soviet Union made the same mistake; they each had a different definition for détente, and this "fatal difference" was ultimately the reason for its demise (Garthoff 1985, 1068). For the Soviets, détente denoted the American acceptance of global parity, while the Americans saw détente as a way of maintaining global superiority in an era when American military and financial powers were relatively limited. Each perceived the other's actions as a betrayal of its own definition of détente, thereby leading to the policy's failure (see Garthoff 1985; Hanhimaki 2000; Westad 1997).

Regardless of their conclusions, a common point of discussion in all these works is the importance of events in the third world, particularly in the swathe of countries that stretched from the Indian subcontinent through the Middle East to the Horn of Africa—a region collectively dubbed the "Arc of Crisis" (Brzezinski 1978, quoted in Halliday 1981, 19). Indeed, an event involving two of these countries featured in perhaps the most famous comment on the failure of détente: in his memoirs, Zbigniew Brzezinski, Carter's national security advisor, stated that détente was "buried in the sands of the Ogaden" (Brzezinski 1983, 189). His point was that Carter's new approach to the cold war was put seriously to the test during the Ogaden War between Ethiopia and Somalia, and there its weaknesses were proven. Such proof then encouraged Soviet adventurism, which further alienated the American public from Carter's attempt to fight the cold war by deemphasizing military power, leading to the withdrawal of the SALT II (Strategic Arms Limitation Talks) Treaty and the collapse of détente.

The purpose of this article is therefore twofold. Although Brzezinski's quote is famous, an in-depth analysis of policy toward the Ogaden War is substantially lacking. For example, Kenneth Morris's biography of Carter makes no mention of the Ogaden; indeed, in their memoirs, although Brzezinski and Cyrus Vance devoted a few pages to events in the Horn, Carter made only passing reference to Africa as a whole (Morris 1996; Schraeder 1994, 13; Brzezinski 1983; Vance 1983; Carter 1982). This article attempts not only to redress this deficiency but also to contribute to the historiographical debate surrounding the era of détente by considering the accuracy of Brzezinski's claim and the responsibility, or otherwise, of the Carter administration in the demise of détente.

The Ogaden War began in August 1977 when, supplied with Soviet arms and reinforced with more than 4,000 Soviet advisors, Mohamed Siad Barré launched an invasion of the Somali-inhabited Ogaden region of Ethiopia. The Somali leader was motivated by irredentism but believed that he could achieve his dreams only through military conquest because of the Cairo Resolution, passed by the Organization of African Unity (OAU) in 1964, which stated that existing borders of African nations would be honored and maintained. Within weeks, with 85 percent of the Ogaden in Somali hands, it appeared that Siad might achieve his aim of merging the region with Somalia (*New York Times* 1977b).

The Ogaden War loomed, according to Paul Henze, the national security staffer responsible for Africa, as the Carter administration's "first foreign policy crisis"[1] and provided a major test of the suitability and credibility of Carter's vision for American foreign policy. Faced with the constraints imposed in the era of the Vietnam War, Carter rejected traditional methods, such as American military power, to fight the cold war. Instead, he chose to emphasize American moral superiority by emphasizing human rights and peaceful resolution of conflict and by focusing upon regionalist, rather than globalist, concerns.

Carter, therefore, limited American involvement in the Ogaden conflict and supported a negotiated settlement to be determined by either the countries directly involved or other African countries—in the administration's regionalist context that African problems should have African solutions (U.S. Department of State 1977, 319), the ideal forum to sponsor negotiations was the OAU. The Policy Review Committee, one of the two subcommittees of the National Security Council during the Carter administration, resolved on August 25 that "we want to try to persuade other Africans to feel a sense of responsibility for what is happening between Ethiopia and Somalia" (Policy Review Committee 1977b) and pledged "to try to get as many African leaders as possible to participate in a call to all outside powers to refrain from supplying arms to fuel the Ethiopian-Somali confrontation so that there can be a cease-fire and an effort at mediation" (Policy Review Committee 1977a).

The OAU officially became involved in the Ogaden War after the Ethiopian government demanded an emergency meeting to discuss Somali aggression. The foreign ministers of eight African nations met in Libreville, Gabon, from August 5 to 9, 1977, but diplomatic skepticism that the talks would fail soon thereafter appeared well founded (*New York Times* 1977d). The Ethiopian delegation insisted that they would never accept the "humiliation" of surrendering part of their territory, and they refused to allow the Ogaden guerrillas to participate in the mediation talks, which led to Somalia's withdrawing from the negotiations. The meeting concluded with a call for the hostilities to cease between Ethiopia and Somalia (*New York Times* 1977a), although because of the Somali withdrawal, this announcement carried little weight. A month after the emergency session had ended, a spokesman for the Ethiopian government pointed out that Somalia had "shown no respect" for the resolution passed by the OAU and clearly "intended to pursue its aggression" (Ross 1977).

Carter also endorsed the standpoint of the OAU that "outside powers should not be 'fuelling' African territorial disputes" and pledged an arms embargo on both sides for the duration of the conflict (Cabinet Meeting 1977). However, the United States's main rival in the cold war did not share Carter's commitment to regionalism and peaceful resolution of conflicts—and the involvement of the

Communist bloc in the Ogaden War posed perhaps the greatest challenge to Carter's new foreign policy approach.

During the first few weeks of the war, the Soviet Union continued to supply military aid to both Ethiopia and Somalia (see Ottaway 1977a; *Washington Post* 1977a; *New York Times* 1977e), but it became increasingly clear that Moscow was choosing sides. In September, the Soviet leadership expressed open disapproval of the Somali incursion (*New York Times* 1977c) and in October took their displeasure a step further by announcing the cessation of all arms supplies to Somalia. The Soviet ambassador to Ethiopia, Anatoly Ratanov, told a news conference in Addis Ababa that Moscow had "officially and formally" terminated military aid to Somalia but was providing Ethiopia with "defensive weapons" to counter the Somali invasion (Benjamin 1977, A27). In addition, the Communist bloc provided manpower to support the Ethiopian troops in the war; on November 5, 1977, the State Department estimated that about 250 Cuban and Soviet military advisors were assisting Ethiopia in the fighting in the Ogaden as well as in Eritrea (the northern province bordering the Red Sea where insurgents had been fighting for independence since the region had been formally incorporated into Ethiopia in 1962) (Hovey 1977).

Siad realized that, if he were to defeat Ethiopian troops backed by Soviet and Cuban might, he too needed external support. This was most likely to come from the West, but presumably only if he no longer had ties with the Communist bloc. Thus, in November 1977, following a 19-hour government meeting, Siad renounced the Treaty of Friendship between Somalia and the Soviet Union; ordered the expulsion of all Soviet military and civilian advisors; and closed the Soviet naval bases on the Indian Ocean, including the base at Berbera (*Time* 1977). At the same time, Siad broke relations with the Soviet Union's ally and perceived proxy, Cuba, and also expelled Cuban diplomats and advisors (*Newsweek* 1977; *Time* 1977). The official government announcement that Siad was breaking these ties was couched in terms designed to elicit Western sympathies by emphasizing the Somali position that Soviet actions were contributing to the repression of freedom. Somali Information Minister Abdulkadir Salaad Hasan charged that the Soviet Union was "brazenly" interfering "in the struggle of the peoples fighting for their liberation from the Ethiopian government" (Wilkinson 1977, A1).

Carter, however, recognized that Siad's ulterior motive in expelling the Soviets was a search for external support and continued to apply a regionalist policy, maintaining the doctrine that outside powers should not fuel the Ogaden conflict. On November 15, the State Department spokesman, Hodding Carter, announced that, despite the Somali action, there would be no change in the administration's policy of refusing to supply arms to Somalia and stated that the administration continued to believe that "African problems should be solved by Africans themselves" (Ottaway 1977b). The determination of the administration to refrain from direct involvement did not please the Somalis, however. At a news conference, the Somali advisor on foreign affairs, Hussein Abdulkador Kassim, declared that "it is the feeling of my Government that the international community has a responsibility to see that the plan of the Soviet Union to destabilize the area is not carried out" (*New York Times* 1977f, 8). The same month Siad called on the United States to "fulfill its moral responsibility" to Somalia. He said he had received "words, just words from the West" instead of material aid, even after expelling the Soviets (*Washington Post* 1977b, A8). However, Carter's new approach to the cold war, and emphasis on regionalism, meant that he saw no reason why the Somalis should expect to be rewarded just because they had expelled the Soviets.

Instead, Carter continued with his attempts to remove Soviet influence from the region. The president shared his concern about the "Soviet Union's unwarranted involvement in Africa" with "the NATO alliance, and specifically with France, the Middle Eastern countries, and India" (Carter 1978a, 57) and also appealed to the Latin American countries, perhaps in the hope that this would influence Cuba. In official communiqués sent to the leaders of various Latin American nations, including the president of Venezuela, Carlos Andres Perez, Carter pointed out that despite American efforts to the contrary, "the Soviet Union and Cuba have become increasingly involved in the Horn, in a way that has transformed a conflict largely limited to regional powers, to one with broader implications and risks" (Carter to Perez 1978). Carter requested that Perez use his influence to "condemn foreign intervention in the internal affairs of another country" (Carter to Perez 1978). The following month, Carter wrote to President Jose Lopez Portillo of Mexico expressing the "deep concern" of the United States over the situation in the Horn, and especially the Cuban involvement, and seeking his "advice on how [to] persuade them to exercise more restraint" (Carter to Portillo 1978).

The administration also expressed its concern directly to the Soviet Union and Cuba. In a meeting with Soviet Foreign Minister Andrei Gromyko in December, Cyrus Vance, the secretary of state, pointed out that the United States supported the OAU position that the major powers should disengage from the Ogaden conflict and added that "it would be useful if the USSR did too" (Vance to Brzezinski 1977). On January 25, Carter sent a letter to Brezhnev seeking Soviet support for a negotiated solution to the Ogaden conflict, based upon respect for territorial integrity, and the "immediate recall of both Soviet and Cuban military personnel from Ethiopia" (Carter to Brezhnev 1978). The following month, a State Department telegram sent via the American Embassy in Cuba requested that the Cuban government also support OAU peace initiatives, pointing out that "continuing Soviet-Cuban involvement will not enhance prospects for such settlement" (U.S. Department of State to U.S. Embassy, Havana 1978).

However, only a year after Carter had entered the White House and inspired new hope for American foreign policy, events in the Ogaden seemed to suggest that his new approach was flawed, as it became increasingly clear that negotiations were unlikely to end the conflict. When meeting with a congressional delegation that Representatives Don Bonker (D-Wash) and Paul Tsongas (D-Mass) led, the Ethiopian leader, Mengistu Haile Mariam, warned that the United States should not "expect the OAU to solve the problem" and contended that the

Somalis would not voluntarily withdraw from the Ogaden. As there was "no force at the disposal of the OAU," it was therefore the "duty of Ethiopia and its armed forces to expel the aggressors" (U.S. Congress 1978c, H462–9). On January 18, 1978, the Ethiopian ambassador to the United States, Ayalew Mandefro, reiterated that the "Ogaden is part of Ethiopia and is not a point of negotiation with Somalia" (*Washington Post* 1978, A16). Neither were the Somalis overly supportive or encouraging about the possible success of negotiations; in an interview, Siad insisted that there was no chance of a negotiated settlement with Ethiopia to end the war over the Ogaden (*New York Times* 1978). Paul Henze, the national security staffer who was responsible for the Horn of Africa, perhaps summed up best the chances for successful negotiation in a memo that he sent to Brzezinski on January 12, commenting that "neither the Ethiopians nor the Somalis want negotiations now; how, then, can you bring them to negotiate? Nor do the Russians and the Cubans want negotiations" (Henze to Brzezinski 1978b).

Indeed, the Soviets seemed dedicated to a military solution to the Ogaden War, and large amounts of Soviet military equipment, plus Communist bloc support in the form of Cuban troops, poured into Ethiopia. On January 23, Henze informed Brzezinski that "between 2,000 and 3,000 more Cuban combat troops are scheduled to arrive in Ethiopia shortly and that planning is well advanced to commit them in the northern Ogaden. . . . The Cuban role is thus rapidly shifting from an advisory one to one of significant involvement in the fighting itself" (Henze to Brzezinski 1978b). On February 23, Admiral Stansfield Turner, director of the CIA, reported that "a Soviet General [Vasiliy I. Petrov] is directing the Ethiopians in battle . . . [and] nearly 10,000 Cubans are in Ethiopia now" (NSC Meeting 1978). Despite the early success that the Somali insurgents enjoyed in the Ogaden, the extent of Communist bloc support for Ethiopia changed the military situation. Henze informed Brzezinski in January that "sometime this year, with all the Soviet weaponry and Cuban help they are getting, [the Ethiopians] are bound to push the Somalis back decisively" (Henze to Brzezinski 1978a).

Well aware of Carter's constant refusals to provide military aid while the war continued, Siad, in his desperation, attempted to depict the conflict in geopolitical terms in a final effort to change Carter's mind. In an exclusive interview with *Newsweek* on February 13, Siad warned that "Russia is outmanoeuvering America" (*Newsweek* 1978), while a senior aide cautioned that "the Soviets can now see the day when they will control the oil supplies and the sea routes of the Western world" (*Newsweek* 1978). Carter, though, maintained his position that the United States would not be pressured into providing Somalia with military aid while the Ogaden War continued; in his memoirs, Vance recalled that "the Somalis were increasingly desperate. Repeatedly, they appealed for U.S. military help as Cuban and Ethiopian pressure mounted. Each time [the Carter administration] asked whether they were prepared to withdraw from the Ogaden. Their answer was no" (Vance 1983, 87).

The might of Soviet and Cuban involvement on the side of Ethiopia in the Ogaden War, added to the lack of international support for Siad, led, almost inevitably, to Somali defeat. On March 9, Carter announced that "last night, I was informed by President Siad of Somalia that he was agreeing to withdraw his forces from the Ogaden area, the occupied areas of Ethiopia" (Carter 1978c, 490). In fact, Siad had little choice in the matter, and the "withdrawal" referred to by Siad was more like a rout. The Ethiopian ambassador to Kenya, Mengiste Desta, told a press conference that the Somali troops were "being chased out from Ethiopian land by [Ethiopian] troops" (Lamb 1978, A1).

Thus, the Ogaden War came to an end. On the surface, it seemed that Carter's policy had borne its promise: there had been no American military involvement, and no American troops had died in another proxy war; the war had ended with the tenets of international law and national integrity fulfilled as the invading army was forced to withdraw; and there had been partial rollback of Communist bloc influence as Somalia broke ties with the Soviet Union and Cuba.

Despite this success, however, Carter's policy was perceived as a failure, arguably because of his inability to "sell" his new approach to the cold war to the American public. Members of the U.S. Congress, in particular, were clearly not convinced by Carter's reorientation of foreign policy and demanded more traditional methods in waging the cold war. As early as October 1977, Representative Robert Sikes (D-Fl) described the refusal of the United States to aid the Somalis as "ineptness" (U.S. Congress 1977a, 35101); and on November 29, he argued that "the United States will be derelict if we do not move quickly to take advantage of the potential" for replacing the Soviet Union in Somalia, particularly in the strategic naval base at Berbera (U.S. Congress 1977b, 38050). On January 19, 1978, Sikes told the House that "I find it exceedingly hard to comprehend an action of the US Government which virtually gives the green light for the conquest of Somalia and Eritrea by Cuban forces under Russian control. . . . Arms for Somalia could have forced a negotiated settlement and kept the strategic Horn of Africa out of communist hands" (U.S. Congress 1978a, 146–47). On February 8, Senator Thomas Eagleton (D-Mo) also expressed his concern about Soviet advances in the Horn, claiming that without U.S. help, "Somalia's relatively small and now-depleted military forces could not meet the military might of Ethiopia's Soviet backed forces, thus assuring a Soviet takeover in the Horn of Africa" (U.S. Congress 1978b, 2664).

In their report to the House Committee on International Relations, following their visit to the Horn, Representatives Bonker and Tsongas also demonstrated a traditional cold war viewpoint. They argued that nowhere on "the African Continent is there an area where the potential for East-West confrontation is greater, or strategic interests more important" (U.S. Congress 1978c, H462–69). The report also invoked the Domino Theory[2] and warned of the dangers of appeasement:

> Soviet strategists have recognized the importance of the Horn of Africa and have shown their willingness to make substantial investments to secure Russia's interests, first in Somalia and now in Ethiopia. By undermining the fragile governments that exist in the Horn, Soviet influence could rapidly spread throughout the region and along the entire East Coast of Africa. . . . As long as there is turmoil and conflict in the Horn of Africa, the United States cannot afford to be complacent. To do so would risk possible Soviet

domination of the whole Indian Ocean area and a consequent threat to fundamental Western interests. (U.S. Congress 1978c, H462–70)

Carter's seeming inability to convince Congress in particular, and the American public in general, that his approach to the cold war was appropriate did not go unnoticed within the administration. In his report on November 18, 1977, Zbigniew Brzezinski warned Carter that although

> the various initiatives you have taken have been right, and individually correct, I feel that we are confronting a growing domestic problem involving public perception of the general character of that policy. To put it simply and quite bluntly, it is seen as "soft". . . . Our critics—will ask for some examples of "toughness," and exploit against us such things as . . . the current Cuban activity in Africa (*NSC Weekly* 1977).

But Brzezinski's concern went further than fears about American public opinion. His priority as national security advisor was American-Soviet relations, and he feared that Carter's approach to the Ogaden War would have a serious impact on that relationship.

Although, in general, members of the Carter administration believed in the rhetoric that human rights should be a concern, that regionalist matters were important, and that the East-West dimension should not be allowed to dominate foreign policy, they also accepted the reality of the world of the 1970s and the fact that American national security concerns necessarily included the relationship with the Soviet Union. The debate that was to plague the administration, particularly in view of media coverage, arose from a difference of opinion over the balance between these two positions. In particular, press attention concentrated upon the relationship between Zbigniew Brzezinski and Cyrus Vance, and although it should be noted that the media often overstated the level of antagonism between the two men, there were key areas in which they differed significantly in their foreign policy outlook. Brzezinski recalled that "we disagreed on a number of issues. We disagreed on Soviet expansionism, we disagreed on how hard we ought to press the Soviets on human rights. We disagreed specifically on the Soviet/Cuban role in Ethiopia and Somalia."[3]

Brzezinski viewed the Soviet Union as threatening and dangerous, and he argued that Soviet actions in the Horn of Africa proved this. In the Special Coordination Committee (SCC) meeting of March 2, 1978, Brzezinski contended that "the Soviets are demonstrating a predisposition to exploit a local conflict for larger purposes. They are frightening more countries in the region and they are creating a precedent for more involvement elsewhere" (SCC Meeting 1978b). In public Brzezinski may have supported the administration's regionalist policy, but in private memos, meetings, and later in his memoirs, it is clear that Brzezinski maintained a more globalist outlook. He argued that "the situation between the Ethiopians and the Somalis was more than a border conflict" (Brzezinski 1983, 178) and warned that Soviet success in the Horn could have serious repercussions around the world. Indeed, parroting classic cold war rhetoric, Brzezinski's report to the president on February 9, 1978, maintained that the Soviet success in the

African Horn demonstrated that "containment has now been fully breached" (*NSC Weekly* 1978a). On February 24, 1978, Brzezinski advised Carter that, unless the United States stood up to the Soviets in the Horn, "we will increasingly find Begin, Brezhnev, Vorster, Schmidt, Castro, Gaddafi, and a host of others thumbing their noses at us" (*NSC Weekly* 1978b). Ten days later, Brzezinski sent a memo to Carter reflecting on the impact of the Soviet's success in the Horn of Africa:

> No one in the region will fail to notice that the Soviet Union acted assertively, energetically, and had its own way. This will have a significant effect on Soviet neighbours; I do not think anyone here appreciates the degree to which the neighbours of the Soviet Union are fearful of the Soviet Union and see themselves as entirely dependent on American resolution. I also do not believe that it is beating the drums of alarm to suggest that in the longer run there will be a ripple effect in Europe as well. (Brzezinski to Carter 1978)

In contrast to Brzezinski's globalist perspective, Vance attempted to adhere to the administration's emphasis on regionalism and, according to Brzezinski, "insisted that this issue [in the Ogaden] was purely a local one" (Brzezinski 1983, 179). Vance argued that the administration should not place too much emphasis on Soviet activities in the Horn and maintained that the Ogaden War had become a "daily crisis" because "we are stirring it up ourselves" (SCC Meeting 1978b). Although it would be wrong to say that Vance took a benign view of the Soviet Union, he did believe that it was possible for the administration to work with the Soviet Union, and his priority, throughout his term of office as secretary of state, was always SALT. For Vance, nothing was more important, and he was determined that nothing should interfere with the talks; at the SCC meeting of March 2, 1978, he warned that losing SALT would be "the worst thing that could happen" (SCC Meeting 1978b).

Thus, debates arose within the administration as to the extent to which other issues should be allowed to impinge on Vance's priority, and the issue of "linkage" became a matter of contention. As Brzezinski recalled

> whether the African problem would be treated purely as an African issue disregarding the Cuban and Soviet involvement and on Rhodesia and South Africa there was agreement between NSC and State that this was a purely African problem. On Ethiopia, Somalia and Angola there was disagreement, the NSC feeling we cannot disregard that since it's part of a larger Soviet policy that therefore affects our larger strategy and the State Department feeling was strongly that now the two issues could somehow or other be compartmentalized.[4]

Notwithstanding internal discussion, the official administration standpoint was that there would be no linkage between various aspects of foreign policy. On February 21, 1978, the SCC "agreed unanimously that there is no direct linkage between Soviet or Cuban actions in the Horn and bilateral activities involving either country and the United States" (SCC Meeting 1978a), and Vance subsequently told a congressional hearing that there was no linkage between events in the Horn and SALT (SCC Meeting 1978b).

However, despite such categorical assertions, in reality the situation was much more complicated, and in practice, some elements of linkage could not be avoided. State Department spokesman Hodding Carter maintained that "as a matter of policy, there is no linkage," but it was inevitable that Soviet actions in the Horn were "going to have a spill over effect in Congress and in the nation as a whole" (Marder 1978, A1). President Carter told a news conference that the administration would never "initiate any linkage," but Soviet activities in the Horn might "lessen the confidence of the American people in the word and peaceful intentions of the Soviet Union, [and] would make it more difficult to ratify a SALT agreement or comprehensive test ban agreement if concluded, and therefore, the two are linked because of actions by the Soviets" (Carter 1978b, 442). Even Vance accepted this fact, acknowledging that Soviet and Cuban involvement in the Horn "cannot help but have an effect upon the relationship between our two countries. It affects the political atmosphere between the United States and those two countries. . . . I am not suggesting any direct linkage, but I do suggest it affects the political atmosphere in which these discussions take place" (U.S. Department of State 1978).

Brzezinski was more blunt when considering the matter of linkage between Soviet activities in the Horn and other aspects of policy. At the SCC meeting on March 2, 1978, he asserted that "if there is an aggravation of tensions because of what the Soviets are doing in the Horn, there is going to be linkage. That is a statement of fact" (SCC Meeting 1978b). Indeed, on January 25, 1978, Carter sent a letter to Brezhnev arguing that Soviet involvement in the Horn "can only breed similar counter-reactions, with unavoidably negative effects on our bilateral relations" (Carter to Brezhnev 1978).

The debates surrounding the deployment of a carrier task force to the Horn also provided evidence of differences of opinions within the Carter administration. The SCC meeting minutes from February 21 noted that the "SCC was divided" over the issue (SCC Meeting 1978c). Brzezinski argued that a task force should be sent because "it is important that regional powers not see the United States as passive in the face of Soviet and Cuban intervention in the Horn and in the potential invasion of Somalia—even if our support is, in the final analysis, only for the record" (SCC Meeting 1978c). However, Brzezinski met with united opposition; in his memoirs, Vance recalled, "every other member of the committee opposed the idea of deploying a carrier task force" (Vance 1983, 87). Brzezinski remembered that "Vance particularly was against any deployment of a carrier task force in the area of the Horn. For the first time in the course of our various meetings, he started to show impatience, to get red in the face, and to raise his voice. I could sense that personal tension was entering into our relationship" (Brzezinski 1983, 182). In this matter, the majority of the SCC, supported by the president, held sway; and the SCC meeting of March 2 noted that "an aircraft carrier will for the time being be kept in the area of Singapore" (SCC Meeting 1978b).

For Brzezinski, this matter was a turning point in the life of the administration. In his memoirs he explained why:

In March 1980, as we were reacting to the Soviet invasion of Afghanistan, I wrote in my journal: "I have been reflecting on when did things begin genuinely to go wrong in the

US-Soviet relationship. My view is that it was on the day sometime in . . . 1978 when at
the SCC meeting I advocated that we send in a carrier task force in reaction to the
Soviet deployment of the Cubans in Ethiopia. At that meeting not only was I opposed
by Vance, but Harold Brown asked why, for what reason, without taking into account
that that is a question that should perplex the Soviets rather than us. The president
backed the others rather than me, we did not react. Subsequently, as the Soviets became
more emboldened, we overreacted, particularly in the Cuban Soviet brigade fiasco of
last fall. That derailed SALT, the momentum of SALT was lost, and the final nail in the
coffin was the Soviet invasion of Afghanistan. In brief underreaction then bred overreac-
tion." That is why I have used occasionally the phrase, "SALT lies buried in the sands of
the Ogaden." (Brzezinski 1983, 189)

But the question remains as to whether Brzezinski was correct to assign such
importance to a conflict in an area of the world that David Lamb of the *Los
Angeles Times* described as a "hot, barren and inhospitable . . . desperately poor
region . . . [with] little economic or strategic value" (1977, B1). In other words, it
arguably mattered little in geopolitical terms who controlled the Ogaden, and it
was Carter's policy in other parts of the world that were more important in influ-
encing Soviet actions.

The most obvious example would be the situation in Iran and the perceived
inability of the Carter administration to free the American hostages held there.
Although Carter brokered the deal that secured the release of the 52 hostages,
the fact that the men were not allowed to leave Iranian territory until Ronald
Reagan took the presidential oath remains the enduring image. There are no
grounds to suggest that the policy of the Carter administration toward the Horn
of Africa prompted the crisis in Iran—it was undoubtedly an issue of religious
fundamentalism and the legacy of American support for the Shah. Similarly, it
appears much more likely that, if the Soviet Union were motivated by the image
of American weakness, it would have been weakness in Iran, rather than in the
Horn of Africa, that gave rise to this crisis.

The decision of the Carter administration to offer full diplomatic recognition
to China, and consent to the seating of the People's Republic in the United
Nations and on the UN Security Council, is also worthy of consideration as an
inducement for Soviet adventurism. Fears within the Kremlin that Soviet influence might be waning in Asia, resulting from the forging of closer relations
between the United States and China, may well have played a part in the Soviet
decision that direct action was needed to bolster its position in other countries in
that region, thereby prompting the 1979 invasion of Afghanistan in support of the
pro-Communist government. Indeed, in his biography of Cyrus Vance, David
McLellan argues that it was Soviet suspicion and concern over the growing Sino-
U.S. closeness, and the implications for Soviet interests in southwest Asia, that
prompted Soviet action in Afghanistan (McLellan 1985, 156). Again, Carter's
policy toward China was unconnected to his African policy, throwing further
doubt on Brzezinski's claim.

Additional evidence that Brzezinski's notion was flawed can be found in quotes
from others during that time. Anatoly Dobrynin, the Soviet ambassador to the
United States from 1962 to 1986, claimed that "from the long-term geopolitical

point of view, the developments in that part of Africa were unmistakably of local importance, and the political leadership in Moscow regarded them as such" (Dobrynin 1995, 403). Thus, if the Kremlin did not attribute any global significance to events in the Horn, it seems unlikely that American actions—or indeed inaction—there affected subsequent Soviet policy toward Afghanistan. This view was shared by Robert Gates, a member of the CIA who transferred to work as Brzezinski's executive assistant from June 1977 to early 1980, before returning to become the director of the CIA during the George H. W. Bush administration. In his autobiography, Gates (secretary of defense during the Obama adminstration) contended that events in the Horn, with regard to either Soviet or American policy, "had no impact on the broader US-Soviet relationship" (Gates 1996, 74).

So détente was perhaps not "buried in the sands of the Ogaden," but the importance of the conflict in the demise of détente should not be underestimated. The war represented the first foreign policy crisis for the Carter administration, and it was here that the president's new approach to the cold war was put to the test. Carter deemphasized American military power and strove for a peaceful resolution of the conflict—but he failed. He invoked the principle of regionalism by insisting that African problems should have African solutions and attempted to remove all outside influence from the conflict—but he failed. Nevertheless, one still might argue that Carter was right, and that the commitment of American military power would have been even worse, both for the situation in the Horn of Africa and for American-Soviet relations.

Notwithstanding, Carter's ultimate failure lay in his inability to convince the American public in general, and the U.S. Congress in particular, that his policy choices were appropriate. Brzezinski claimed that, because of the Ogaden War, "the momentum of SALT was lost," and he was correct, but it was not the Soviet momentum that was most important in 1978; it was American public opinion. Perhaps Carter's handling of the Ogaden War emboldened the Soviets, but ultimately it was the willingness of the American people to support SALT, not the support of the Soviet Union, that was undermined by Carter's handling of the conflict in the Horn of Africa. As Brzezinski noted in his report to the president in November 1977 (*NSC Weekly* 1977), the Ogaden War raised doubts among the American people, which were exacerbated by international events throughout Carter's administration and consolidated by the Soviet invasion of Afghanistan. Subsequently, Carter withdrew SALT from Senate consideration, and the era of the second cold war began.

In conclusion, let us consider how this analysis fits into the historiographical debate surrounding the demise of détente. Carter's foreign policy, whether in 1977 or 1980, was designed to improve the status of the United States in the international environment, suggesting that Halliday's focus on the American role might be most accurate. However, Carter was not acting in an aggressive way, and it could certainly be argued that his policy choices were responsive to the limits on American power that were apparent during his administration. Indeed, given that Carter's ultimate failure was his inability to convince the public to maintain its support for SALT, this suggests that the way that Carter handled the Ogaden crisis seems more emblematic of the historiographical school of thought advanced by Odd Arne Westad (see Westad 1997).

Discussions of Carter's failure to engage public opinion also feature in historiographical evaluations of Carter's presidency as a whole. Some offer this as further evidence of Carter's weakness as president; Gaddis Smith, for example, acknowledged that Carter's vision of foreign policy was "morally responsible and far-sighted" but argued that he failed to communicate this effectively to the American public because of his inability to successfully lead his administration or manage Soviet adventurism (Smith 1986, 247). However, this analysis of Carter's policy toward the Ogaden War supports strongly the view of those analysts, including Jerel Rosati, who, while crediting Carter with a coherent worldview, argue that the president's failure to gain public support lay with the rising tide of conservatism in the United States (Rosati 1994). Indeed, it could be argued that public sentiment in the mid-1970s, which enabled Carter's election and facilitated his initial foreign policy approach, was a temporary aberration: an immediate reaction to Vietnam and Watergate, but one that quickly passed. The conservative right in the United States demanded a tough foreign policy, but Carter was perceived as a stereotypical Democratic president, one who was "soft on Communism"[5] (Ringle 1978, A17); his policy toward the Ogaden War was but one element, albeit an important element, in creating this perception. Ultimately Carter failed in convincing the American people to support his vision because he, similar to many Democrats subsequently, was unable to combat the trend toward Republicanism in American politics—a trend that arguably began with the election of Richard Nixon in 1968; spawned the 1994 Republican Revolution, when Republicans seized control of both houses of Congress for the first time in 40 years; and continued into the twenty-first century.

Events in the Ogaden region of Africa are therefore important to historians of the cold war for many reasons. This study has offered, for example, further insight into the limitations on foreign policy formulation in the era of the Vietnam War and a greater understanding of some of the internal dynamics within the Carter administration, particularly the relationship between Brzezinski and Vance. Perhaps most important, though, is the significance of the Ogaden War to the demise of détente. Although the "ownership" of this region in Africa was arguably unimportant to the overall balance of power between the United States and the Soviet Union in the cold war, the perception of American weakness in the face of Soviet strength had a profound impact on the way that the Carter administration was viewed by the American public. As Brzezinski claimed, the momentum of SALT was severely undermined by events in the Ogaden, with serious repercussions for both Jimmy Carter, who failed in his bid for reelection in 1980 largely due to his image as weak and ineffective, and the subsequent development of the cold war.

Notes

1. Paul B. Henze, conversation with author, April 1999.

2. "Domino Theory" refers to the idea that if one country were to become Communist, then, like a row of falling dominoes, its neighbors would be likely to follow.

3. Interview with Zbigniew Brzezinski, National Security Advisor to the Carter Administration, 6 July 2000, Center for Strategic and International Studies, Washington D.C.

4. Ibid.

5. In August 1978, the Republican governor of Virginia, John Dalton, announced his intention to "send the message, all over this state, that the Carter administration is soft on communism." See Ringle (1978).

References

Benjamin, Milton R. 21 October 1977. Soviets halt supply of arms to Somalia; West faces dilemma. *Washington Post*.

Brzezinski, Zbigniew. 1983. *Power and principle: Memoirs of the National Security Adviser, 1977–1981*. New York, NY: Farrar, Straus, & Giroux.

Brzezinski, Zbigniew to Jimmy Carter, memo. 3 March 1978. Zbigniew Brzezinski Donated Historical Material, Carter Presidential Library.

Cabinet Meeting. 1977. Minutes from 12 September 1977. Plains File, Carter Presidential Library.

Carter, Jimmy. 1978a. President's News Conference, 17 January 1978. In *Public papers of the presidents of the United States: Jimmy Carter 1978 volume I*. Washington, DC: Government Printing Office.

Carter, Jimmy. 1978b. President's News Conference, 2 March. 1978. In *Public papers of the presidents of the United States: Jimmy Carter 1978 volume I*. Washington, DC: Government Printing Office.

Carter, Jimmy. 1978c. President's News Conference, 9 Mar. 1978. In *Public papers of the presidents of the United States: Jimmy Carter 1978 volume I*. Washington DC: Government Printing Office.

Carter, Jimmy. 1982. *Keeping faith: Memoirs of a president*. London, UK: Collins.

Carter, Jimmy to President Carlos Andres Perez of Venezuela. 19 January 1978. Zbigniew Brzezinski Donated Historical Material, Carter Presidential Library.

Carter, Jimmy to President Jose Lopez Portillo of Mexico. 13 February 1978. WHCF Countries (CO), Carter Presidential Library.

Carter, Jimmy to Leonid Brezhnev. 25 January 1978. Plains File, Carter Presidential Library.

Dobrynin, Anatoly. 1995. *In Confidence: Moscow's Ambassador to American's six cold war presidents (1962–1986)*. New York, NY: Random House.

Garthoff, Raymond. 1985. *Détente and confrontation: American-Soviet relations from Nixon to Reagan*. Washington, DC: Brookings Institution Press.

Gates, Robert M. 1996. *From the shadows: The ultimate insider's story of five presidents and how they won the cold War*. New York, NY: Simon & Schuster.

Halliday, Fred. 1981. *Soviet policy in the arc of crisis*. Washington, DC: Institute for Policy Studies.

Halliday, Fred. 1986. *The making of the second cold war*. London, UK: Verso.

Hanhimaki, Jussi. 2000. Ironies and turning points: Détente in perspective. In *Reviewing the cold war: Approaches, interpretations, theory*, ed. Odd Arne Westad. London, UK: Frank Cass.

Henze, Paul to Zbigniew Brzezinski. 12 January 1978a. NSA Staff Material, Carter Presidential Library.

Henze, Paul to Zbigniew Brzezinski. 23 January 1978b. NSA Staff Material, Carter Presidential Library.

Hovey, Graham. 5 November 1977. U.S. says Cuban advisor unit in Ethiopia tripled. *New York Times*.

Lamb, David. 1 August 1977. Claimed by 2 nations: Ethiopia's Ogaden: New battleground in Africa. *Los Angeles Times*.

Lamb, David. 12 March 1978. Ethiopia rejects Somali bid for ogaden peace. *Los Angeles Times*.

Mardar, Murrey. 2 March 1978. U.S. Links SALT fate, Horn of Africa. *Washington Post*.

McLellan, David. 1985. *Cyrus Vance*. Totowa, NJ: Rowman & Allanheld.

Morris, Kenneth E. 1996. Jimmy Carter, American moralist. Athens, GA: University of Georgia Press.

Newsweek. 28 November 1977.

New York Times. 9 August 1977a. Ethiopia now talks of full-scale war.

New York Times. 4 August 1977b. Somalia says guerrillas attack Ethiopia defences.

New York Times. 30 September 1977c. World news in brief: Brezhnev criticizes Somalia over fighting.

New York Times. 5 August 1977d. World news in brief: Ethiopia says Somalia controls many areas.

New York Times. 24 September 1977e. World news in brief: Major battle in Ogaden foreseen by diplomats.

New York Times. 10 December 1977f. World news in brief: Somali says Soviet aim is instability in Africa.

New York Times. 30 January 1978. World news in brief: Somali leader rules out negotiated settlement.

Newsweek. 13 February 1978. The battle for the Horn.

NSC Meeting, Minutes. 23 February 1978. Zbigniew Brzezinski Donated Historical Material, Carter Presidential Library.

NSC Weekly. 18 November 1977. Report no. 37. Zbigniew Brzezinski Donated Historical Material, Carter Presidential Library.

NSC Weekly. 9 February 1978a. Report no. 46. Zbigniew Brzezinski Donated Historical Material, Carter Presidential Library.

NSC Weekly. 24 February 1978b. Report no. 8. Zbigniew Brzezinski Donated Historical Material, Carter Presidential Library.

Ottaway, David. 7 August 1977a. Moscow on tightrope in Somali-Ethiopia dispute. *Washington Post*.

Ottaway, David. 15 November 1977b. U.S. applauds Somali decision to expel Soviets. *Washington Post*.

Policy Review Committee. 1977a. Minutes from 25 August 1977. Zbigniew Brzezinski Donated Historical Material, Carter Presidential Library.

Policy Review Committee. 1977b. Summary of Conclusion from 25 August 1977. Zbigniew Brzezinski Donated Historical Material, Carter Presidential Library.

Ringle, Ken. 20 August 1978. Va. GOP message: Carter soft on communism. *Washington Post*.

Rosati, Jerel. 1994. The rise and fall of America's first cold-war foreign policy. In *Jimmy Carter: Foreign policy and post-presidential years*, ed. Herbert Rosenbaum and Alexej Ugrinsky. Westport, CT: Greenwood.

Ross, Jay. 8 September 1977. Ethiopia breaks ties with Somalia. *Washington Post*, A22.

SCC Meeting. 1978a. Minutes from 21 February 1978. National Security Archives, Washington DC.

SCC Meeting. 1978b. Minutes from 2 March 1978. Zbigniew Brzezinski Donated Historical Material, Carter Presidential Library.

SCC Meeting. 1978c. Summary of Conclusions from 21 February 1978. Zbigniew Brzezinski Donated Historical Material, Carter Presidential Library.

Schraeder, Peter J. 1994. *United States foreign policy toward Africa: incrementalism, crisis and change*. Cambridge, UK: Cambridge University Press.

Smith, Gaddis. 1986. *Morality, reason and power*. New York, NY: Hill & Wang.

Time. 28 November 1977. Horn of Africa: Russians, go home!

U.S. Congress. 1977a. Representative Sikes (D-Fl), speech on 25 October 1977. *Congressional Record*. Washington, DC: Library of Congress.

U.S. Congress. 1977b. Representative Sikes (D-Fl), speech on 29 November 1977. *Congressional Record*. Washington, DC: Library of Congress.

U.S. Congress. 1978a. Representative Sikes (D-Fl), speech on 19 January 1978. *Congressional Record*. Washington, DC: Library of Congress.

U.S. Congress. 1978b Senator Eagleton (D-Mo), speech on 8 February 1978. *Congressional Record*. Washington, DC: Library of Congress.

U.S. Congress. House. 1978c. *War in the horn of Africa: A firsthand report on the challenges for United States policy*. 95th Congress, 2nd Session. H. Doc. 462–9. Washington, DC: Library of Congress.

U.S. Department of State. 1977. Philip Habib, statement on 4 April 1977. *Department of State Bulletin* 76, no. 1971. Washington, DC: Library of Congress.

U.S. Department of State. 1978. Secretary of state's news conference, on 10 February 1978. *Department of State Bulletin*, 78, no. 2012. Washington, DC: Library of Congress.

U.S. Department of State to American Embassy, Havana. 10 February 1978. NSA Staff Material, Carter Presidential Library.

Vance, Cyrus. 1983. *Hard choices: Critical years in America's foreign policy*. New York, NY: Simon & Schuster.

Vance, Cyrus to Zbigniew Brzezinski. 12 December 1977. Zbigniew Brzezinski Donated Historical Material, Carter Presidential Library.

Washington Post. 22 September 1977a. Ethiopians said getting Mig-21s from Soviets.

Washington Post. 29 December 1977b. Somalia says two towns hit by Ethiopian planes.

Washington Post. 19 January 1978. Ethiopia, promising counteroffensive, tells West not to enter Somali fight.

Westad, Odd Arne, ed. 1997. *The fall of Détente: Soviet-American relations during the Carter Years*. Oslo, Norway: Scandinavian University Press.

Wilkinson, Raymond. 14 November 1977. Somalia orders Soviet advisors out. *Washington Post*.

Decolonization or National Liberation: Debating the End of British Colonial Rule in Africa

By
CHEIKH ANTA BABOU

When discussing the end of British colonial rule in Africa, many historians have highlighted the role of postwar international relations and the impact of domestic imperial politics on decolonization and have failed to recognize the role of African nationalists. This article argues that such a viewpoint is flawed because it conceives of colonial policy makers as isolated and autonomous entities impervious to changes taking place in the colonies. The national liberation movements in Ghana, Central Africa, Kenya, and other regions of East Africa are explored in this article to illustrate the central role that colonial subjects played in the British decolonization of Africa. While dominant scholarship on the failures of the post-colonial state has made studies of decolonization and African nationalism less fashionable, it is becoming increasingly clear that our understanding of the nature and mechanics of the crises that beset the continent requires taking fresh stock of the record of European colonial rule in Africa. In this regard, the study of colonialism and decolonization in Africa continues to be of critical relevance.

Keywords: decolonization; colonial rule; Africa; British Empire; federalism; Ghana; Kenya

In the aftermath of the Second World War, European empires in Africa faced insurmountable challenges. The internal and external conditions that sustained colonial rule were unraveling at an extraordinary pace. As one commentator aptly noted, the European colonial regimes could continue to exist only so long as three requirements were fulfilled: (1) that their colonial subjects acquiesced in their authority,

Cheikh Anta Babou teaches African history and the history of Islam in Africa in the Department of History at the University of Pennsylvania. His research focuses on mystical Islam in West Africa and Senegal and on the new African diaspora. He has published extensively on the Muridiyya Muslim order of Senegal and the Senegalese diaspora. In 2007, he published Fighting the Greater Jihad: Amadu Bamba and the Founding of the Muridiyya of Senegal, 1853–1913 *with Ohio University Press. His articles have appeared in journals such as* African Affairs, Journal of African History, Journal of Religion in Africa, *and* Africa Today.

DOI: 10.1177/0002716210378647

(2) that the politicians and electorates of the metropolitan countries accepted colonial commitments as not entirely unethical and on the whole worthwhile, and (3) that these empires received international recognition (Gifford and Louis 1988). While recognizing the critical importance of these three factors in determining the fate of colonial rule, most historians of decolonization in Africa have emphasized postwar international relations and the impact of domestic imperial politics on decolonization and have discounted the role that the colonial subjects played. The reasons for decolonization, they argued, resided in the anticolonial sentiments of postwar U.S. and Soviet administrations and the deliberate planning of enlightened colonial bureaucrats and politicians in London and Paris. The impact of nationalist pressure was deemed insignificant; even in places such as Ghana, where the role of Kwame Nkrumah could not be ignored, it was the liberal policy of the Colonial Office in London that was credited with paving the way for African democratic expression and, ultimately, for the achievement of Ghana's independence in 1957. Thus, the planned decolonization thesis championed by Ronald Robinson and John Flint emerged as the dominant narrative of British decolonization in Africa (see Flint 1983; Robinson 1980).

The problem with this argument, mostly made by British scholars of imperialism working with Colonial and Foreign Office archives in Europe, is that it conceives of colonial policy-makers as isolated and autonomous entities impervious to changes taking place in the colonies and motivated solely by their political idiosyncrasies and metropolitan considerations. It fails to consider how the new international order was affecting African perceptions of colonial rule and overlooks the important impact that nationalist leaders, the rising political consciousness of the colonial subjects, and intensifying protest movements in the colonies were having on policy-makers in London. In reality, what was presented as planned policies for decolonization appeared more as bricolage aimed first at anticipating African political demands, second at containing those demands when they were not anticipated, and third at finding ways for preserving British interests when decolonization became inevitable. This contention becomes clear when we look at the processes and mechanics for the dissolution of the British colonies of West, East, and Central Africa, but it is important that we first consider the nature of international relations during and after WWII, changes taking place in the colonies, and the role that these events may have played in precipitating the end of colonial rule.

The End of the Colonial Empires in Africa

One major consequence of WWII for colonized people in Africa and elsewhere was that it destroyed France's and Britain's entrenched confidence that there would be no serious external challenge to their imperial authority. Even before the end of the war, at the different conferences held by the Allies at Potsdam, Yalta, and San Francisco and at the drafting of the Atlantic Charter, a new international order had dawned in which the former imperial powers were no longer able to play leading roles. The greatest threat that this new international order posed to Britain was that it could potentially put its colonies under international scrutiny and eventually out of its control.

The newly founded United Nations and its emphasis on human rights and the rights of self-determination for all nations provided a new international forum that undermined the discretionary policies of the imperial powers and helped to build an international consensus against colonial rule. The internationalization of the colonial problem had already started with the founding of the League of Nations after the First World War, the creation of the mandate system, and the introduction of the notion of trusteeship in the language of international politics. The establishment of the international community as legal custodian of the Ottoman and German colonies, in the Middle East and Africa, respectively, created a juridical precedent that undermined the rights of conquest, which, since the Berlin Conference in 1885, had served as legal framework for colonial rule. It also introduced a moral dimension in the colonized–colonizer relationships and imposed some measure of accountability on Britain and France, which were entrusted with the administration of mandate colonies. These two countries were expressly tasked, as laid out by Chapter XII of the UN Charter, "to promote the political, economic, social, and educational advancement of the inhabitants of the trust territories, and their progressive development towards self-government or independence as may be appropriate to the particular circumstances of each territory and people."[1]

Of course, all of these generous stipulations existed only on paper, and the UN often failed to muster the will and the means to turn them into real policies. In the end, the mandate system did not affect, in any meaningful way, the administration of African subjects. There were no major differences in the everyday lives of subjects in mandate and nonmandate colonies in the manner in which colonial administration was carried out. But from a political standpoint, the new international status afforded colonies under UN supervision larger room for political maneuver. In due time, nationalists in Tanganyika, Togo, and Cameroon would take advantage of this opportunity to oppose British and French policies and advocate for special treatment. Accommodations made to satisfy the demands of mandate colonies in turn influenced policies in other colonies.

The emergence of the United States and the Soviet Union as dominant postwar powers presented another major obstacle to colonialism and an opportunity for Africans to achieve self-rule. Both of these countries, for different reasons, appeared at least initially as natural allies of the people in Africa and Asia struggling to overthrow the yoke of European imperialism. The United States, a former colony that fought for its own independence (although it also experimented with colonial rule in the Philippines and the Pacific Islands), was by character and temperament drawn to anticolonialism; also, as a new economic superpower, its interests lay in equal access to the natural resources and markets of European colonies.

Although the influence of communist ideas on Africa south of the Sahara in the postwar era was rather limited, and the disruption of colonial rule in Africa never became a priority for Stalin, the Soviet Union was nevertheless another threat to colonial tranquility. Yet aside from diplomatic efforts to embarrass the colonial powers in the UN and other international fora, in Africa this threat would unfold only in the 1960s and 1970s in the heat of the cold war and the wars of liberation in Portuguese colonies. It is revealing that none of the early nationalists who helped to pave the way to independence in Africa professed to be communist, although there is no doubt that they were all influenced by Marxist ideas about class struggle, capitalism, and imperial exploitation.

While changes in international relations brought about by WWII exerted some pressure on the colonial powers, their impact should not be overstated. The new international political and diplomatic environments alone could not have prompted European imperial powers to give up their colonies. In fact, as noted by Anthony Low, "international pressures on colonial powers could be irritants. But the ease with which the Portuguese and Smith regimes brushed them aside for so long serves to underline their ineffectiveness" (Low 1988, 70). It was the political, economic, and cultural changes that were taking place on the African continent before, during, and after the war that had an even greater impact on the process that led to the end of colonial rule in Africa.

World War II fundamentally impacted the existing relationships between African subjects and their colonial masters. Both those who were forced to fight in the battlefields of Africa, Asia, and Europe, as well as those who stayed on the continent toiling in the mines and farms to support the war effort, were deeply affected by their experience. Colonies were mobilized as critical resources to fund the war. In many colonies, cut off from the metropolitan capitals for the first time, emphasis was put on developing local productive capacities and not just on extracting raw materials. These economic changes allowed a small minority of Africans to fill low- and middle-level manufacturing and office jobs vacated by European conscripts or made available by the war industry, but the war economy was mostly felt in the colonies, which reverted again to forced labor. This practice was extensively used in British, Belgian, and French colonies, such as Côte d'Ivoire, Congo, and Kenya, to produce record harvests of agricultural products and extract mineral resources, such as copper, uranium, and iron, necessary for the military industry. The pressure put on the farmers to intensify the cultivation of cash crops needed for hard currency and to feed the swelling urban population and the soldiers on the front lines created famines and anger throughout Africa. These hardships became the face of colonialism even among people in rural areas whose lives had not been fundamentally affected by colonial rule.

Political maturity was even greater among the many Africans who were forcibly drafted into the colonial armies, where they served in various capacities such as combatants, cooks, porters, and drivers. In many instances, for these Africans who fought alongside their European counterparts or visited the European metropolises, the war experience helped to destroy many of the myths associated with European power. The war humanized the European master. The myth of invincibility cultivated by Europeans in the colonies was forever buried in the battlefields of Europe, Asia, and Africa. Soldiers who were deployed in the devastated cities of Europe—filled with beggars and the wretched—and who were sometimes called for duties of population control learned that Europe also had its poor people and its share of misery. Overall, as observed by one historian, "for many African soldiers, the experience of fighting side by side with European soldiers in the war had a tremendous formative impact, expanding their world view and forcing them to question their subject status and the professed benevolence of their overlords. These Africans gained confidence that they could influence their own destinies if they were willing to take action, make sacrifices, and struggle for what they wanted" (Keller 1995, 158–59). As we shall see in the following pages, WWII veterans were instrumental players in the nationalist movement.

The aftermath of the Second World War was also marked by a growing demand for more formal education and for a greater role for Africans in the economy and administration of the colonies. This was particularly the case in urban areas. Africans who had profited from the extraordinary circumstances of the war by carving out a niche in the colonial economy held high expectations that their lives would continue to improve after the war. Formal education was thought of as a primary means to achieve social mobility.

The vociferous demands for better education and greater roles for Africans in the political, administrative, and economic lives of the colonies sent a strong signal to the colonial rulers that it was no longer possible to conduct colonial business as usual. The imperial metropolises in Europe clearly understood the message but still believed that there were ways of repairing and revamping the colonial system. They were determined to breathe new life into colonialism by inventing a new legitimacy for colonial rule. This new political orientation started what some historians have called the "the second colonial invasion." Now the declared intentions of colonialists were to substitute counsel for control, to modernize Africa, and to share more equitably the costs and benefits of economic development. New economic plans were drawn in London and Paris, and even some of the money from the Marshall Plan intended for European reconstruction was committed to funding projects on the African continent. In Britain, economic investment was channeled through the successive Colonial Development and Welfare Acts of 1945, 1950, and 1955. Specialists, mostly Europeans, were recruited to implement new policies for agricultural production and marketing, to provide new social and medical services, and to work in fisheries or education. African labor was sought to staff larger projects geared toward improving communication, power, and water supplies.

Postwar development plans also included an important educational component. Britain trained a new African elite mainly in high schools and colleges built on the continent such as Achimota in Ghana and Makerere in Uganda. The new institutions of higher education were tasked with preparing the future leadership of Africa by gradually Africanizing the workforce in the colonies.

Political reform was another important dimension of postwar colonial policy. In the British colonies, it had become clear that indirect rule and its reliance on customary chiefs to control the population had outlasted its political usefulness. Now emphasis was put on the development of an "efficient and democratic system" of local government that would require all those aspiring to a seat in the legislative and executive bodies of administration in the colony to go out and compete with local candidates. Yet this reform was not solely motivated by the declared intention of "sowing democracy in African minds." Colonial policy-makers and administrators branded radical nationalists as demagogues motivated by their own selfish interests and out of touch with the majority of their countrymen who appreciated the modernizing benefits of colonial rule (Cooper 2005, 26). Colonial officialdom hoped that the entanglement in local politics would deflect nationalists from operating on the national level and ultimately dim their rising popularity.

The new effort to reform colonial rule, rather than assuage the discontent and demands that motivated its implementation in the first place, achieved just the opposite. Post–WWII economic and political reforms in the colonies exposed clearly to the public the deep-seated contradictions that lay at the heart of the colonial project. As noted by some scholars of decolonization, "European imperialism embodied a fundamental tension between the desire to represent the colonized as innately different . . . and the need to consider them sufficiently alike as to make the effort worthwhile" (see Nugent 2004, 11).[2] African nationalists shrewdly exploited these contradictions. On one hand, they insisted that they were the same as the Europeans and therefore entitled to the same political rights. On the other hand, "they had recourse to a rich field of cultural symbolism which underlined their essential difference from the Europeans and which could be used as [a] rallying point" (Nugent 2004, 11). The Négritude movement pioneered by Aimé Césaire of Martinique and Léopold Senghor of Senegal in the 1930s in Paris constitutes a good illustration of this contention (see Césaire 1956; Senghor 1963). Frantz Fanon's work put an even greater emphasis on the deep political meaning and psychological impact of European cultural alienation (see Fanon 1967). Imperial response to these contradictions was a gradualist approach, which no longer excluded the prospect of African self-government but instead hoped to push it back to an indeterminate future. The true goal for reform was to find ways of preserving the empire, but it soon became clear that any attempt to delay or stem political and social transformation in the colonies would breed anger and frustration and that nationalists' demands could not be satisfied or contained in the framework of improved local government (Hargreaves 1988, 109).

The Undoing of the British Empire in Africa

In the aftermath of WWII, while India was firmly on the path to political sovereignty and Britain was contemplating that for Middle Eastern colonies, the Colonial Office in London still believed that self-government for West Africans was decades away and that the prospect for East and Central African colonies was even more remote. African nationalism proved to have no respect either for the timeline that colonial bureaucrats drew or for the distinction made between West Africans and other colonies. By 1951, distinctions between different stages of local autonomy, between self-government and independence, and between politically advanced and less advanced colonies had become increasingly irrelevant, especially in nonsettler colonies.

Events in the Gold Coast colony, later the Republic of Ghana, set in motion the British scramble for decolonization. There, in 1947, the United Gold Coast Convention (UGCC) was formed by nationalist members of the bourgeoisie as a political instrument to expedite the progress toward self-government, and Kwame Nkrumah was hired as its general secretary. Nkrumah was a staunch Pan-Africanist and nationalist who had spent 12 years abroad studying and traveling in the United States and Europe and meeting with political activists from across the British Empire. He was a prominent participant in the Manchester Pan-Africanist Congress of 1945 organized by W. E. B. Du Bois, which articulated clearly the demand for total sovereignty for the European colonies in Africa and outlined a strategy to attain it. Nkrumah's readings and experience had taught him the critical importance of a centralized and disciplined political party that could identify needs and establish roots in the urban and rural areas of the country. Soon he presented to the founders of UGCC detailed proposals to achieve just that.

The critical event that led to the undoing of the British Empire in sub-Saharan Africa took place in Accra, Ghana, in February 1948, when the police fired shots and killed two Ghanaian former servicemen involved in a veterans' protest. The killing led to rioting and looting in the city that spread to three other towns; eventually 29 people died. Nkrumah and five leaders of UGCC were quickly rounded up and then released. This event was a traumatic warning to the colonial administration that it was losing the political initiative to the nationalists and prompted Sir Hugh Foot, the British chief secretary in Nigeria, to note that "the most important thing is to take hold of the initiative [and] and not allow frustration to set in" (Low 1988, 39). The commission formed to enquire into and report on the disturbances in the Gold Coast and their underlying causes articulated sharp criticism of almost all aspects of colonial government in the colony and concluded that "in the conditions existing today in the Gold Coast substantial measure of reform is necessary to meet the legitimate aspirations of the indigenous population" (Hargreaves 1988, 116). But time was already running out for reform, and it would soon become clear that the pace and nature of changes to come would not be determined by colonial bureaucrats in London but by nationalists in Africa.

In 1949, Nkrumah and his followers broke away from UGCC to form the Convention People's Party (CPP). The following year, they embarked on a campaign of "positive actions," reminiscent of Gandhi's campaign of civil disobedience, to demand "self-government now." Strikes and violence ensued, followed by a declaration of a state of emergency and the arrest of Nkrumah. Despite the successful suppression of the positive actions campaign, keeping Nkrumah in prison was not an option. He had come to embody the aspirations of the Ghanaian people for self-government. Short of violent conflagration in the colony, which the British wanted to avoid at all cost, they had no alternative but to engage him. Furthermore, constitutional reforms adopted in hopes of bolstering moderate political forces failed as the CPP swept the election of 1951, winning 34 of 38 elective seats. Charles Arden-Clarke, the new governor of the Gold Coast, who had some experience negotiating with nationalists in Southeast Asia, released Nkrumah from jail. Without delay, Nkrumah became the Gold Coast's leader of government business and later prime minister. Britain was now set on a constitutional course to grant self-government to Ghana, and the subsequent victories of the CPP in the elections of 1954 and 1956 convinced them that independence could not be delayed or denied any longer. In 1957, the Gold Coast achieved independence under the new name of the Republic of Ghana.

Once independence was conceded to Ghana, it could not be denied to Nigeria, the largest British colony in sub-Saharan Africa, where there was already a burgeoning nationalist movement. But the size of Nigeria and the religious and ethnic entanglements of nationalist politics there dictated a different pace. The preservation of the emirate in the northern part of the country through the policy of indirect rule had largely restricted access to Western education and kept this area immune to outside political influences. The southwestern and southeastern provinces dominated by the Yoruba and Igbo ethnic groups, in contrast, had long benefited from mission education and greater contacts with the outside. The influence of Pan-Africanist ideas, already perceptible there in the 1930s, underlines the extent to which southern intellectuals were connected to the wider Atlantic World.

Nigerian politics in the run-up to independence was dominated by three regional political blocs: Nnamdi Azikiwe's party, the National Council of Nigeria and the Cameroons (NCNC), based in the east with a mainly Ibo constituency, but aspiring for nationwide presence and influence; the Action Group (AG), the party of Obafami Awolowo, which mobilized the Yoruba ethnic group in the west; and the latecomer, the mainly Muslim Northern People's Congress (NPC), which was supported by the large population of Fulbe and Hausa in the north of the country. Because of cultural and political differences among these three regions and the particular intellectual itineraries of the leadership, the three parties showed significant differences in their approaches to decolonization and their perception of the future of the colony of Nigeria. When, in 1943, the AG introduced a motion to the Federal Legislative Council for self-government by 1956, the NPC refused to back it and threatened secession of the Northern Province. Faced with a crisis that might have led to a violent confrontation, the British brokered a new constitution in 1954. This constitution devolved significant decision-making powers to the Nigerians but also gave its imprimatur to the de facto division of the country by shifting the center of the federation to the three ethno-religious regions. This meant that the political voices of the dozens of other minority ethnic groups were ignored and that the north, with a population larger than that of the west and east combined, could achieve permanent control of the country if it managed to muster political cohesion. Finally, after nationally held elections in 1959, power was transferred to a shaky coalition of the NPC and the AG. Britain's failure to address correctly the minority question in its rush to decolonize portended fatal consequences for post-colonial Nigeria: the Biafran War between 1967 and 1970 and the continuing struggle more than 40 years after independence to solve the conundrum of ethnic nationalism. After the independence of Nigeria, the smaller colonies of The Gambia and Sierra Leone soon followed.

The contention that events unfolding in Africa rather than colonial planning in London dictated the pace and trajectory of decolonization is even more evident in the case of the British colonies of East Africa (Kenya, Uganda, Tanganyika) and Central Africa (Nyassaland, Southern Rhodesia, Northern Rhodesia). In 1959, an influential official in the Colonial Office estimated that Kenya could not expect independence until 1975 (Goldworthy 1970, 278). For Central African colonies, independence was forecast decades after West Africa and envisioned only in the framework of a federation.

In the views of colonial officials, five major reasons explain the special treatment reserved for the British East and Central African colonies: the presence of a demographically small but economically and politically powerful white settler community, the need for economic integration of the different colonies if they were to stand a chance of survival, pressure from the racist Republic of South Africa, the lack of a strong and well-educated class of intellectuals ready to lead the country after independence, and the absence of strong nationalist movements.

Unlike West Africa, all British colonies in East, Central, and Southern Africa incorporated white settlers. These Europeans were successful in wresting substantial political and economic privileges from the imperial state. As early as 1923, the white population (nearly 200,000 in the 1950s) of Southern Rhodesia (current-day Zimbabwe) had largely secured internal self-government. In Kenya, where the settler community was even smaller (130,000 in 1950), the settlers, nevertheless, succeeded in acquiring a special status by forcing the abandonment of the principle of equal representation envisioned in 1948 in the High Commission and Legislative Assembly. Throughout East and Southern Africa, settlers adamantly opposed the notion that universal suffrage might be applicable to Africans, at least for the foreseeable future. They saw themselves as rightful trustees of the majority black population. As noted by Paul Nugent, they were "fixated on the discourse of perpetual colonialism and to a substantial degree they enjoyed the backing of local administrations" (Nugent 2004, 31). What was offered to the Africans was multiracialism in a political system that established parity of representation at both the center and lower levels of administration among blacks, Asians, and Europeans, regardless of demographic weight. This offer was regarded by dismayed African nationalists as an attempt to perpetuate white minority dominance.

Along with the idea of a so-called multiracial partnership, federalism was another argument concocted to satisfy settler aspirations through concealed rhetoric about economic efficiency. As observed by one noted historian in the case of Central Africa, "Many who supported Federalism as a road to independence did so precisely because it would exclude the danger of Black Power which was now raising its head in West Africa" (Hargreaves 1988, 135). Federalism was conceived as a means of combining the complementary strengths of the different East and Central African colonies' economies and reducing the cost of administration. In the East African case, it was argued that a closer union among Kenya, Uganda, and Tanganyika would make the vast population of farmers in the two latter colonies benefit from the skills and know-how of Kenyan white settlers. In Central Africa, the backers of federalism pursued two major aims: the creation of a viable state sympathetic to imperial policy and the combination of the economic assets of the three colonies. The plan was to combine the rich mineral resources of Northern Rhodesia with the labor reserve of Nyassaland and the entrepreneurial skills of the Southern Rhodesian white population. What was not said and what African nationalists clearly understood was that the unification of the colonies would also consolidate the white settler population and give them an even greater power in the administration and economy of the future federations.

Across East and Central Africa, multiracialism and federalism met staunch opposition from Africans. In Tanganyika, the opposition to multiracialism and federalism was led by Julius Nyerere and his political party Tanganyika African National Union (TANU). This colony was particularly targeted as a land of immigration for white Europeans in the post-WWII era. In the decade after 1948, its white population doubled from 10,648 to 20,598, and these settlers benefited from the political arithmetic of racial parity, which gave them 10 representatives in the Legislative Council on par with 80,000 Asians and 8 million blacks (see Hargreaves 1988, 132; Nugent 2004, 32). Already in 1929, the suggestion of a closer union among the British East African colonies had led to the formation of the African Association, which was the first political party with national coverage in Tanganyika. In response to the postwar plans to make good on the projects of multiracialism and federalism, Nyerere transformed the African Association into the more cohesive and better organized TANU in 1954. He was able to capitalize on mounting discontent in urban and rural areas, which was spawned by attempted reorganization of local government and heavy-handed agricultural improvement schemes. Emulating the example of Nkrumah, Nyerere was highly successful in building youths' and women's branches of the party and in weaving a web of supporters across the colony. He also skillfully played on the special status of Tanganyika as a UN trusteeship to Britain. This status set limits to what the British could impose on Tanganyika, while providing Nyerere with an international forum sympathetic to his demands. Here, as in Ghana, the colonial administration leveraged loyal political forces in an effort to undercut the nationalist movement by sponsoring the multiracial party, United Tanganyika Party (UTP). But when elections were held in 1958–1959, UTP fared badly and thereafter disappeared from the political scene. In 1959, a conference of East African governors proposed a timetable for decolonization, with 1970 as the date for ultimate transfer of power. TANU rejected the proposal, and when they swept the first nonracial elections of 1960, conceding only one seat to their competitors, the British government had no choice but to bow to the demand for immediate independence. Full independence was granted in 1961 with Nyerere as head of the new state.

In Kenya, Britain faced perhaps its most traumatic experience of decolonization in Africa. Here the combination of population growth, especially among the Kikuyu, postwar settler immigration, the scarcity of available agricultural land for

Africans, and ill-fated economic improvement projects created an explosive mix that detonated with the Mau Mau rebellion between 1952 and 1956.

From 1924 on, political organizations, such the Kikuyu Central Association (KCA) founded by Harry Thuku, were formed to articulate local grievances and to defend the economic and cultural interests of the Kikuyu people. But it was not until the founding of the Kenyan African Union (KAU) in 1944 that an attempt was made to organize an African political party with territorial ambitions. This party was formed by the mainly Nairobi-based elite, many of whom worked for the colonial government. The party benefited from the fact that it was the only nationalist party in Kenya at the time. And expectations were heightened when Jomo Kenyatta, returning from London, assumed the party's presidency. Kenyatta had been in Europe for 15 years, mainly in England, where he earned a university degree as an anthropologist and wrote the first academic interpretation of Kikuyu culture (*Facing Mount Kenya*). His political career had started earlier as a member of KCA, which he joined in 1924 before becoming its general secretary in 1928.

Kenyatta returned to Kenya in 1946 as the best-educated and most sophisticated African politician of the colony. Under Kenyatta's leadership, up to 1952, the KAU continued to articulate the same grievances of past associations: the restitution of land that Europeans had stolen, the increase of African representation in the different levels of colonial legislative bodies, the recognition of equal elective representations with Europeans and ultimately full control, the restriction of European and Asian migration, the end of restrictions on Africans' access to the civil service, and finally, the abandonment of spatial discrimination (Maloba 1998, 57). The failure of the colonial state to act on these grievances discredited the gradualism advocated by the proponents of constitutional nationalism in KAU and opened the door for frustrated Kenyans to act.

In 1951, strikes by low-paid workers had caused violent confrontations in Nairobi. Ex-servicemen, the so-called Forty-Group, landless squatters displaced by settler expansion, and radical trade unionists infiltrated KAU and radicalized the organization, sidelining the moderate elite. They formed a new central committee and adopted the Kikuyu tradition of oath taking as a tool to build loyalty among their followers. By mid-1952, the colony experienced an outbreak of arson, cattle maiming, and targeted violence aimed mainly at Kikuyu supporters of official colonial policies and white settlers. The disturbances were so violent that the administration lost control over much of the Kikuyu land, which was the epicenter of the events. A state of emergency was imposed, and Kenyatta, who openly dissociated himself from the violence and its perpetrators, was thrown in jail. The colonial state was able to restore order only after four years of intense fighting in the forests and protracted guerilla operations against an elusive enemy they called Mau Mau but who branded themselves as the Land and Freedom Army. In the end, 2,000 Africans, 32 Europeans, and 26 Asians lost their lives in the war. Historians have disagreed in their assessment of the objectives of the leaders of the Mau Mau and the meaning of the movement, but it is safe to note, as Paul Nugent does, that "it would be difficult to maintain that African opposition was anything other than the crucial factor here, even if nationalism assumed an ethnic form" (Nugent 2004, 35). By 1956, after peace was reestablished, Britain was seriously reconsidering its options in Kenya. In a now-familiar pattern, the colonial administration engaged in an effort to find moderate nationalists who would be willing to strike a deal with moderate settlers to preserve imperial interests. But the effort failed as none of those who enjoyed popular African support took the risk to accept a settlement that might reenforce settler power. Finally, under nationalist pressure, Britain agreed to release Kenyatta from prison and grant independence under majority rule. In 1963, Jomo Kenyatta was elected the first president of independent Kenya.

The last blow to multiracialism and federalism came from African and white nationalists in the Central African Federation. Because of the threat represented by South African imperialism, white settlers in Central Africa enjoyed a stronger bargaining position than their counterparts in East Africa. In the run to independence, they could trade their loyalty to the British Empire for political and economic concessions. The establishment of the Central African Federation, regrouping the two Rhodesias and Nyassaland, owed much to the pressure white settlers exerted on the Colonial Office in London. But by the 1950s, the makeshift partnership between the African constituency and white settlers was under growing stress. First, the promise of economic betterment that underpinned the federalist idea was slow to materialize for Africans, especially in the poorer colony of Nyassaland. It was the white population who monopolized the modern sector of the economy, especially in Southern Rhodesia, that most benefited from imperial investments and subsidies. In 1957, when Britain advanced the idea of granting dominion status to the Central African Federation, Africans were alarmed. For them, this meant the removal of British oversight and the prospect of permanent white settler domination akin to what was going on in South Africa. African nationalists were further disturbed when the Colonial Office refused to heed an amendment by the African Affairs Board aimed at blocking discriminatory voting regulations, which, if enacted, would give the whites de facto control of the Federal Assembly.

This situation clearly highlighted the complicity between the imperial government and the white settlers, galvanizing African nationalists. There was now a rapid acceleration of nationalist activity both in the urban and rural areas and the emergence of a political leadership ready to organize and channel the discontent toward achieving self-government. The Zambia National Conference was formed in Northern Rhodesia in 1958 by Kenneth Kaunda. In the same year, Dr. Hastings Banda returned to Nyassaland, after a 40-year absence to study in the United States and Europe, to lead the Congress Party, in existence since the 1940s, in its fight against the federal constitution. Both Kaunda and Banda were among Nkrumah's guests during the All-African People's Congress in 1958. In 1959, popular protests broke out throughout the federation in the form of strikes and riots. States of emergency were declared and nationalists were arrested. But these events convinced colonial officials that the settlers would be able to hold power over Africans only through massive use of force; furthermore, if delaying the process of decolonization was to invite violence, then premature independence and the transfer of power from Europeans to Africans was preferred. After elections were won by the same nationalists who were imprisoned, the British government agreed to dissolve the federation. In 1964, the Central African Federation ceased to exist. Nyassaland became independent as Malawi under the leadership of Banda, while Kaunda took power in Northern Rhodesia, renamed Zambia. In Southern Rhodesia, it was the white population that issued a Unilateral Declaration of Independence in 1965 with the support of South Africa, but they soon confronted a war of national liberation led by Joshua Nkomo and Robert Mugabe, who succeeded in ending white minority rule in 1980. And Southern Rhodesia was renamed Zimbabwe.

Conclusion

The study of colonial rule and decolonization has largely gone out of fashion, as the dismal record of the post-colonial African leadership, whether revolutionary or accommodationist, has dimmed the enthusiasm of progressive historians, who worked hard in the 1960s and 1970s to establish African nationalism's role in ending European colonial rule in Africa. Now corruption, genocide, refugees, civil wars, military coups, and ethnic conflicts have become the favored topics of historians and social scientists studying Africa. But while the outbreak of these scourges owes a lot to the ineptitude and corruption of the post-colonial African leadership, it is becoming increasingly clear that unsolved problems bequeathed by the colonial state continue to cast a long shadow on modern African nations.

The economic and political viability of many African countries in their inherited colonial borders is being questioned. The emergence of ethnic nationalism in many areas constitutes a challenge to the centralized national state inherited from colonial rule. The continuing influence of the colonial state's authoritarian modes of operation enshrined in colonial-era constitutions and laws provides the foundation and justification for bad governance today. The great disparity in natural resources between neighboring states, as is the case between the Democratic Republic of Congo and Côte d'Ivoire and their neighbors, is now seen as a potential source of violent conflict, and calls are being made for the sharing of resources across national boundaries. While the presentist orientation noted in the scholarship on African politics remains critical in our understanding of the nature and mechanics of the crises that beset the continent, the resolution of all these problems requires taking fresh stock of the record of European colonial rule in Africa. In this regard, the study of colonialism and decolonization in Africa continues to be of critical relevance.

Notes

1. See the United Nations Charter, International Trusteeship System, Article 76. Available from http://secint50.un.org/en/documents/charter/chapter12.shtml (accessed 19 September 2009).

2. Nugent is commenting here on the works of Whomi Bhabha and Partha Chatterjee.

References

Césaire, Aimé. 1956. Culture et colonisation. *Présence Africaine* 8–10:190–205.

Cooper, Frederick. 2005. *Colonialism in question: Theory, knowledge, and history.* Berkeley, CA: University of California Press.

Fanon, Frantz. 1967. *Black skin, white masks.* Trans. Charles Lam Markmann. New York, NY: Grove Press.

Flint, John. 1983. Planned decolonization and its failure in British Africa. *African Affairs* 82 (328): 389–411.

Gifford, Prosser, and W. M. Roger Louis, eds. 1988. *Decolonization and African independence: The transfers of power, 1960–1980.* New Haven, CT: Yale University Press.

Goldworthy, David. 1970. Conservatives and decolonization: A note on the interpretation by Dan Horowitz. *African Affairs* 69 (274): 278–81.

Hargreaves, John D. 1988. *Decolonization in Africa.* New York, NY: Longman.

Keller, Edmond J. 1995. Decolonization, independence, and the failure of politics. In *Africa*, 3rd ed., ed. Phyllis Martin and Patrick O'Meara, 156–71. Bloomington: Indiana University Press.

Low, Anthony. 1988. The end of the British Empire in Africa. In *Decolonization and African independence: The transfers of power, 1960–1980*, ed. Prosser Gifford and W. M. Roger Louis, 33–72. New Haven, CT: Yale University Press.

Maloba, Wunyabari O. 1998. *Mau Mau and Kenya: An analysis of a peasant revolt.* Bloomington: Indiana University Press.

Nugent, Paul. 2004. *Africa since independence.* New York, NY: Palgrave.

Robinson, Ronald. 1980. Andrew Cohen and the Transfer of Power in Tropical Africa, 1940–1951. In *Decolonization and after: The British and French*, ed. W. H. Morris-Jones and Georges Fischer, 50–71. London, UK: Frank Cass.

Senghor, Léopold Sédar. 1963. Négritude and the concept of universal civilization. *Présence Africaine* 18:9–13.

Radical Islam in East Africa

By
CHARLES R. STITH

Islam has a 1,000-year history in West Africa; in East Africa it is even longer. What started out as liberating efforts by Muslims in Africa degenerated into oppressive regimes over time. Over the centuries, conquest increasingly came to define Islam's approach in Africa. How Africa manages its necessity to accommodate Islamic elements in its midst is one of the continent's most daunting challenges. On the one hand, the region is home to a substantial number of Muslims. On the other hand, there is a connection between religious radicalism and poverty. Tanzanian President Jakaya Kikwete, a Muslim, suggested that if belief is the potential seed of radicalism, then poverty is the fertilizer. Overcoming the factional divide within Islam is important because the fissures are latent in countries with large Islamic populations. How Africa manages this challenge has profound long-term implications for peace, stability, and development on the continent.

Keywords: Islam; radicalism; poverty; Africa; peace; stability

Onone month after I was confirmed as the U.S. Ambassador to Tanzania in 1998, al Qaeda bombed the U.S. Embassy there and in Kenya. One month after the bombings, I assumed my post. Needless to say, for the 2.5 years that I was in Tanzania, I thought a lot about terrorism and the impact of radical Islam in East Africa. Because of my work at Boston University, I continue to follow these issues.

From my perspective, the conventional wisdom that Tanzania and Kenya were hit because

Ambassador Charles R. Stith holds a faculty appointment in the Department of International Relations at Boston University and is the director of the African Presidential Archives and Research Center (APARC). His op-eds have appeared in the International Herald Tribune *and the* Boston Globe. *He is the author of* For Such a Time as This: African Leadership Challenges *(APARC 2008) and* Political Religion *(Abingdon Press 1995). He is a member of the Council on Foreign Relations.*

NOTE: Portions of this article first appeared in the Fall 2006 edition of *The Ambassadors Review*, published by the Council of American Ambassadors. © Charles R. Stith

DOI: 10.1177/0002716210378676

they were "soft targets" did not seem to add up. There were a number of reasons why I came to this conclusion. At the time of the bombing, very few American embassies met the security standards later set by the Crowe Commission.[1] That is to say, in short, almost all American embassies were "soft targets." There were any number of U.S. missions outside of Africa that could have been attacked that would have given al Qaeda greater bragging rights and more political fodder than the attacks against Tanzania and Kenya.

Relative to Tanzania, in particular, there were a number of other factors that cut against the "soft target" theory. First, from the liberation era to the end of apartheid, Tanzania provided safe haven for almost every liberation movement in Africa and beyond. Second, its founding president, Julius Nyerere, was one of the leaders of the nonaligned movement during the cold war years. Last, given the neighborhoods in which the embassies were located and the composition of the workforces at the embassies, there could have been no doubt that the attacks would result in exponentially more Africans than Americans being killed. These factors, along with the ease with which other, higher-profile embassies could have been attacked, would seem to have exempted Tanzania from this sort of assault. The only issue on which Tanzania could be considered vulnerable, given al Qaeda's ideological bent, was its "friendship" with the United States. Ergo, the conclusion that the bombings at U.S. embassies in Africa were not only about terror but about territory—territory in the sense of shrinking America's field of influence. Africa, in this case, was simply a pawn in a hegemonic game of radical Islamists extending their influence and joining the battle against America in another theater. It was against this backdrop that I started to look more closely at the issue of political Islam and Africa.

One of the first things I came to appreciate during my studies was that there is a history here. It is a history reflecting a clear record of hegemonic incursions by Arabs and Islam in Africa. In the earlier years, the contact was less about conquest. Islam has a 1,000-year history in West Africa. In East Africa, it is even longer, reflecting the trade patterns of the dhow countries, which include the Arabian Peninsula, Pakistan, India, and East Africa. Over the centuries, conquest increasingly came to define Islam's approach in Africa. Prior to the present jihad against America, there were five other jihads. Two were launched in Africa:

> After the first centuries of the creation of the Islamic states, there were only four widespread uses of jihad as a mobilizing slogan—until the Afghan jihad of the 1980s. The first was by the Kurdish warrior Saladin in response to the conquest and slaughter of the First Crusade in the eleventh century. . . . The second widespread use was in the Senegamiba region of West Africa in the late seventeenth century. . . . The third time jihad was widely waged as a "just war" was in the middle of the eighteenth century in the Arabian Peninsula, proclaimed by Muhammad Ibn Wahab. . . . The fourth widespread practice of jihad as an armed struggle was in the Sudan when the anticolonial leader, Muhammad Ahmed (1844–1885), declared himself al-Mahdi (the Messiah) and began to rally support against a Turko-Egyptian administration. (Mamdani 2004, 51–52)

In both cases, what started out as liberation efforts by Muslims in Africa degenerated into oppressive regimes over time. That Africa would be a strategic location for radical Muslims to spread their ideology is reflective of a larger historical pattern. Islamists have demonstrated a historical comfort in treading through African soil on the way to a "greater cause," or in violating African sovereignty as a "larger prize." Both reasons would explain radical Islam's threat to African sovereignty and stability.

The historical precedents aside, there are current causes to explain Islamic fundamentalists' encroachment on the continent. On one hand, Africa is home to a substantial number of Muslims.[2] Because of the large number, the statistical probability that there are going to be some radical elements among the population is obvious, if for no other reason than chance. On the other hand, there is a connection between radicalism and poverty. Clearly, the causes of religious radicalism are more complex than its connection to poverty—Osama bin Laden, the scion of a wealthy Saudi businessman, being a case in point. But, duly noting this, it is the Western world's disparate treatment and impoverishment of Muslims that influences the calls to arms that leaders, such as bin Laden, issue. In a speech at Boston University, on September 25, 2006, sponsored by the center that I head, Tanzanian president Jakaya Kikwete, a Muslim, underscored this connection. He suggested that if belief is the potential seed of radicalism, then poverty is the fertilizer. He said,

> Poverty seems to push people closer to their religions for protection, services, and material needs when the communities or government units in their areas cannot provide these amenities. This would be okay if it ended there. If this reaction is intensified it may have disintegrative effects in the communities and then at the level of the nation. In other words, poverty tends to disintegrate people from the larger territorial community only to integrate them in their community of believers.
>
> This is how poverty indirectly affects nation-building. It affects democratization as well. Democracy, human rights, etc. mean little to a hungry person. Researchers have cited cases of poor people who have sold their voting cards during elections for amounts equivalent to one or two meals. More disturbing, however, is the potential for poor people being recruited by global terrorist movements of a religious or secular nature. What I am saying is that poverty can destroy all that we have achieved at the national or global level, and therefore it should continue to be addressed seriously at both levels.

For historical and contemporary reasons, Africa is fertile soil for fringe elements of Islam to take hold. The problem radical Islam poses for Africa is neither abstract nor isolated; there are clear and present dangers all across the continent.

In addition to the Dares Salaam Nairobi bombings, and the threat to East Africa and the Horn has been reflected in other ways. The longest civil war on the continent, which devolved into genocide, has taken place in Sudan. When the settlement to end the war was negotiated in Addis Ababa in 1972, all of those involved agreed that the war pitted Arabs (Muslims) of the north against the Africans (Christians) of the south. It is inarguable that this divide partly defines the genocide that took place in the country.

Somalia is another flashpoint in the Horn. At present, Islamist militias control Mogadishu. Somali leaders appealed for international assistance to help to protect the country from what was purported to be an extension of the al Qaeda network.

While it is unclear the extent to which al Qaeda might have infiltrated the country, the CIA pursued leads on three Somalis believed to have been involved in the 1998 al Qaeda bombing of the U.S. Embassy in Tanzania as well as of the U.S. Embassy in Kenya (Weiser 2000). Further complicating the picture in Somalia, and the Horn of Africa, is the assessment by some analysts that if Somalia falls to radicals, war with Ethiopia is imminent (Adow 2006).

Historic smuggling routes that run from Pakistan to the Comoros Islands and down to Mozambique and Madagascar are well known to terrorist elements. These routes have been navigated skillfully, as evidenced by the fact that this was probably the entry point for materials used for the Dar/Nairobi bombings and most recently by pirates marauding along this same corridor.

Since 1998, radical Islamists have kept Kenya in their crosshairs. In November 2002, Mombasa, Kenya, was attacked by al Qaeda, using a car bomb to blow up the Israeli-owned Paradise Hotel. Eighteen people died in the incident. Simultaneously, the same forces were involved in an unsuccessful attempt to take out an Israeli airliner with surface-to-air missiles.

As active as these groups have been in East Africa, particularly in the Horn, efforts to extend their hegemony are not limited to this region. The threat of al Qaeda is a reality in West Africa. Donovan Chau, an American authority on terrorism, notes,

> The threat of al-Qaeda in West Africa is primarily through its use of the subregion as a financial source and transit point. Notable transportation nodes include Kotoka International Airport in Accra, as well as the ports of Tema and Sekondi, all in Ghana. An example of the use of West Africa as a transit point occurred in 2005, when South African national Farhad Dockrat was detained in The Gambia for suspected terrorist activity and identified as having provided nearly $63,000 to al-Akhtar, a charity that was designated in 2003 for providing support to al-Qaeda. (Chau 2008, 28)

There have been other direct links to al Qaeda in Mauritania and Mali (Radio France International 2009), with attacks against the military in the former and kidnap attempts of French citizens in the latter (Agence France Presse 2010). To the south, in Nigeria, the sectarian violence that has convulsed that country has its roots in religious extremism. Though the upheaval in the Delta region is construed as being about oil, both the impetus and money can be tied to those with Islamic fundamentalist leanings.

Finally, Africa's southern region has suffered radical Islam's wrath. In the aftermath of the bombing of Planet Hollywood in Cape Town, the irony should not be lost that because of the African National Congress's history with groups such as the PLO, Hamas, and Hezbollah, Islamic radicals have had ready access to South Africa. That access has been used to exploit the country's banking system to bankroll their operations around the world. There are reports "that South African passports are finding their way to al-Qaeda operatives worldwide" (Agence France Presse 2010, 41).

After the embassy bombing, I had any number of conversations with African politicians and diplomats in Tanzania about what happened and their sense of what it meant. It became clear to me that a "dirty little secret" that no one wanted to discuss openly was political Islam's corrosive effect and adverse impact on development and stability on the African continent. It is inarguable that Islam is a factor in Africa. The only question is whether there are strategies and tactics that might mitigate (or, at least, neutralize) any potential adverse impact. This question is one that requires a response within the continent and outside of it.

The need for a response within the continent is rather obvious. Overcoming the factional divide within Islam is important in countries with large Islamic populations. Dealing with those virulent strains so as not to weaken the body politic is critical. The political and economic dynamic, simply put, is about stability and development. A house divided against itself cannot stand, it cannot attract investment, and it cannot develop a consensus relative to the end game of growth and development. A specific example of how terrorism impacts Africa economically is the fallout from the 1998 bombings on tourism. In the immediate aftermath of the bombings, the U.S. Department of State issued travel advisories for both Kenya and Tanzania, the point of which were to discourage visits by U.S. tourists to either country. An analysis of tourism in East Africa, commissioned by the World Wildlife Fund, noted that while the factors affecting tourism are complicated and complex, in the years following the bombing there was a clear downturn in tourism in the East African region. Terrorism certainly had to be considered a factor (Nelson 2007).

Though not obvious, the response from outside the continent is as necessary for a number of reasons. The emergence of political Islam, as we know it, was a response to Western power (Nelson 2007, 14). Its evolution is a reaction to Western hegemony. A fundamental lesson of 9/11 is that distance is no arbiter of political Islam's impact on the West. Thus, wherever these radical strains exist, the way in which they are mollified, modified, or mitigated is fundamental to ensuring Western security.

Africa is an area of the world where American interests are most vulnerable and where there is one of the best opportunities to defend and propagate the values that are the underpinnings for democracy and the free market. The threat to U.S. interests in Africa is real. The fingerprints of bin Laden and his cohorts are visible all over the African continent.

Almost half of the FBI's twenty-five most wanted for attacks against American interests are from African countries. In addition to Egypt and Libya, they come from such places as the Comoros Islands, Zanzibar, and Kenya. The effort—by those such as the *maitasine*[3]—to institute Sharia law in the northern provinces of Nigeria is nothing less than an effort to "Talibanize" the country. All of the players that have fomented problems elsewhere—in Sudan, Libya, Iran, and Pakistan—have been present in the northern provinces of Nigeria. A foiled 2009 Christmas Day plot by al Qaeda to blow up an airliner bound for Detroit, Michigan, began in Lagos, Nigeria. In addition to physical threats to America, there is the economic threat this movement presents. Nigeria is a major source of American oil; should these extreme factions gain control of the pipelines, there is a risk that the spigots could be shut off at any time.

Immediately after 9/11, a Mauritanian national was detained in Berlin because of suspected direct ties to those involved in the suicide plot. There are reports (see *Africa Confidential* 2002) from Tanzania that Muslim extremists (the *wanaharakati*) have dedicated themselves to seizing control of the 487 mosques in the Dar es Salaam region. One source asked to distinguish between the local groups and al Qaeda said, "They are the same people everywhere." Should something like this happen, it would most certainly affect the current friendship between the United States and Tanzania.

People against Gangsterism and Drugs (PAGAD) in South Africa has suspicious connections to al Qaeda and was declared a terrorist group by the U.S. Department of State in the aftermath of 9/11. Hussein Solomon of the International Institute for Islamic Studies noted, in a paper produced by his institute, that the bombing of Planet Hollywood in South Africa in August 1998 was an

> act of terror [that was] ostensibly retribution following a U.S. attack on Sudan. This constituted the first terror attack on South African soil as a result of external variables it could not control. In 2009, this sequence of events was to be repeated following the U.S. killing of a senior al Qaeda operative Saleh Ali Saleh in Somalia. According to media reports, intercepted cell phone communications indicate a Somali group, with links to al Qaeda, planned to attack various U.S. interests in South Africa in revenge for Saleh's killing. As a consequence, the U.S. embassy, consulates, and the offices of the U.S. Agency for International Development closed for two days. In both cases, this most recent plot, as well as the Planet Hollywood bombings, the target of the group's rage was the U.S. as opposed to South Africa. Inevitably in such attacks, however, it is not the U.S. which suffers but ordinary [South Africans]. (Solomon 2009, 1)

Sudan, as has been well documented, is a former retreat and staging ground for bin Laden. Were these direct links not enough to make the point that Africa is vulnerable to fanatical elements of Islam, logic would suggest that there ought to be some concern. In light of the significant amount of attention that the United States and its allies are paying to the Middle East and Far East, and the extent to which Europeans are focusing on terrorists in their midst, there are few places that these people might find safe haven. Under these circumstances, Africa would certainly be one of them.

Africa and America, as well as the West in general, have a mutual interest in overcoming the threat that radical Islam poses to them. That there is a cost for African governments that do not take on fanatical forces that have demonstrated their willingness and intent to destabilize and subvert African governments is indisputable. Taking these elements on is easier said than done. What needs to be appreciated is that quite often these fanatical elements operate from relative positions of strength in the countries in which they are present. They draw their strength from several sources: (1) constituencies within the countries where they have set up shop; (2) the extremists' argument that Western capitalism is not the answer to Africa's problems (with the exception of Mauritius, the promise of capitalism to provide economic prosperity has not been fulfilled in these countries); (3) the history of Western exploitation and neglect as a propaganda edge (the West exploited billions of dollars in human and natural resources from Africa during the colonial period and spent billions during the cold war to destabilize African countries and thwart development, with the aim of furthering Western hegemony); (4) the ways in which countries—such as those in East Africa—mitigate the impact and influence of these forces within their borders (this does not necessarily translate into a secure environment for the United States—9/11 is the proof of the pudding); and last, (5) the fact that many of the Islamist organizations or countries that the United States (and West) label as terrorists—Hezbollah, Hamas, Libya, and Iran—were staunch allies of African liberation movements when those movements were similarly labeled. In this vein, people forget that it was not until Nelson Mandela was elected president of South Africa that he was officially dropped from the U.S. terrorist watch list. What all of this means is that mutual interest does not necessarily translate into a common cause. The context and character of the challenges that Africa faces in dealing with radical Islam and terrorism are very different. African governments must weigh the question of whether it is in their interests to work with (and how closely should they work with) the United States and others in dealing with this problem.

America cannot break the backs of organizations such as al Qaeda without the help of governments in Africa. While in Tanzania, I saw firsthand how invaluable African intelligence assets were to the investigation of the U.S. Embassy bombings in Africa. Without the help of the Tanzanians and the South Africans, the United States would not have captured K. K. Mohamed, the only person tried, convicted, and incarcerated for the Dar bombing.

The challenge for the West, and the United States in particular, is how to make it more beneficial to be a friend of rather than indifferent to Western interests. To say it differently, the challenge is to raise the level of Western engagement in Africa such that the "cost-benefit ratio" makes it worth the while of Africans to combat these forces because it is mutually beneficial. Simply put, to engage at such a level from a U.S. perspective means our seeing African economic security as relevant to U.S. national security. Historically, this has not been the case, even when the United States was most heavily involved in Africa during the cold war. A CIA operative confessed, "We have never been in Africa to report on Africa. . . . We went into Africa as part of the covert activity of the cold war, to recruit (as spies) Soviet, Chinese, Eastern European, and sometimes North Korean officials under circumstances that were easier to operate under than in their home countries" (Chau 2008, 10). With the establishment of United States African Command (AFRICOM), the first unified command solely dedicated to U.S. security interests in Africa, this has changed. The question is whether this is sufficient. Even though defense and development are AFRICOM's dual mandate, I would say no, it is not enough.

There are a number of things, both general and specific, that need to be done. Pro forma, the U.S. government needs to check in with those African countries with which it has good bilateral ties and that are "natural" allies because of their commitment to democracy and free market economies to determine the extent to which both are threatened by the same hostile forces and then plan appropriate countermeasures. The United States is doing this to some extent with initiatives such as the International Law Enforcement Academy (ILEA) in Gabarone, Botswana, to counter crime, including terrorism; and the U.S. Treasury Department's program, also based in Gabarone, to combat money-laundering and terrorism-financing schemes (Chau 2008, 19). In East Africa there is the East Africa Counter-Terrorism Initiative (EACTI), which is funded by $100 million to provide counterterrorism equipment, training, and assistance as well as teacher training and community outreach to six countries—Djibouti, Eritrea, Ethiopia, Kenya, Tanzania, and Uganda (Chau 2008, 20). In West Africa there is the Gulf of Guinea Guard initiative aimed to assist ten countries[4] in the Guinean basin beef up maritime security to enable these countries to fend off drug and weapons trafficking and terrorists, for example (Chau 2008, 13–14). While all this might seem impressive at first blush, it is not enough. The tilt of what the United States has done so far has been toward defense. More needs to be done on the development side. This is not to say that the defensive aspect of America's counterterrorism strategy needs to be deemphasized. The strategy simply needs to be equal parts defense and development. The United States needs to look for ways to help its African allies to shore up the public- and private-sector institutions that will enable them to fight off the assaults on the nascent societies that they are trying to create. In the main, that means doing several things.

Aid. One of the most cost-effective counters to fanaticism is aid. I am not talking about aid as we know it at present. The NEPAD (New Partnership for Africa's Development) project's entire agenda to further democracy and free market reform in Africa could be underwritten for $64 billion a year. While this obviously falls short of the need, the United States's (and the West's) financial support could accomplish some very important things. More important, such support validates the "partnership" between the West and Africa, and it is partnership that is the key to success in the battle against terrorism. In addition, this figure is far less than military expenditures to fight fanaticism at present in the U.S. budget. Another critical area to which increased aid could be directed is education. Not only is an educated citizenry necessary for a country to compete in a global market that is driven by technology, but secular schools provide educational alternatives to the *madras*, the religious schools that are incubators for fanaticism and do little to assist in the skill development that is necessary to combat poverty (McGirk et al. 2003).

Trade policy. With all of the talk about the necessity for free and open markets, it is important for the West to do more than "talk the talk"; we must "walk the walk." In 2000, Western countries provided $245 billion in subsidies to their farmers. Not only is this five times the total development aid that the West provided to the rest of the world, it clearly puts farmers in developing countries at an extreme competitive disadvantage in the global marketplace. Our prohibitive industrial tariffs also contribute to the lack of open markets in the West. We need to move forward with free trade agreements with those African countries moving toward democracy and free market reform.

I have highlighted these recommendations because they offer the most immediate bang for the buck. A more detailed agenda for engagement is contained in George B. N. Ayittey's contribution in this volume, "The United States and Africa: A Revisit."

Beyond the United States's "aid and trade" focus I have suggested, another specific way for America to make a statement about its resolve to stand firm in the face of Islam's encroachment in Africa is its involvement in Darfur. The Bush administration led the way in calling the catastrophe in Darfur what it is—genocide. It is important that the United States take the next steps. Given the extent to which the United States is overextended in Iraq and Afghanistan, America is highly unlikely to send troops to the region. But if the United States is as serious as it says it is about stopping the genocide in Darfur, provisions need to be made to provide the necessary resources for the African Union peacekeepers to enforce that peace and rein in the reign of terror of the Sudanese government. The United States cannot continue fiddling around over who will provide and pay for UN peacekeepers while innocent women, children, and men are literally, and figuratively, allowed to burn.

Americans were told in the aftermath of 9/11 that the strategy to defend and protect America would be far-reaching. But in reality, those efforts have not reached far enough. It is not enough to focus on the Middle East and the Far East. It is not enough to focus on developing the right military strategy, perfecting our intelligence technology, and building up our security infrastructure. One key is to develop friends for the long haul, so that America is not in the position of befriending leaders and countries in the short term that do not share its values.

In a speech to graduates at the United States Military Academy at West Point in 2002, then-President George W. Bush implicitly affirmed the need for a broader strategy when he stated that there are terrorism cells in close to one-third of the countries of the globe. A military strategy on all these fronts is not only impossible but also inappropriate. In other words, America must rise to the diplomatic challenge because the only real and lasting antidote to fanaticism is claiming the moral high ground on the "values and vision thing" and alleviating poverty and the discontent that incubate it. What better place to make a primary theater for this fight against fanaticism than in Africa, where a substantial number of leaders have declared that they are ready, willing, and able to fight for democracy and free market reform, at home and abroad?

For America, it is essential to the United States to engage Africa in the fight against terrorism. Concomitantly, I would argue that it is critical for Africa to enlist Western assistance in its fight against terrorism. Africa needs everything from the technology to the intelligence that the West brings to the table. While such assistance (and collaboration) is critical to mitigating the influence and impact of radical Islam in Africa, even more important are the initiatives that Africans undertake. As was implied in the recommendations for action by the United States (and other countries in the West), there is no silver-bullet solution to the problem of terrorism in Africa. Neither radicalized elements nor their potential recruits can be blown out of the water. The process to limit the reach of radical Islam will be painstaking and must be deliberate. Some tactics are obvious, but none are quick and easy.

First, African leaders must openly address and define the problem. This is critical to exposing subversive and spurious arguments radical groups might use to undermine governments and enlist disaffected citizens in their causes. These groups flourish in a vacuum. The lack of a response validates their arguments and causes. Each radical element has to be confronted individually, to be sure, but the overarching ideology of these groups has to be dealt with as well. Exposing and opposing these elements is critical to building a counterconstituency.

Second, in addition to the ideological battle, there are practical challenges in responding to grassroots issues such as poverty. In summarizing Tanzanian President Jakaya Kikwete's assessment of this problem, I made the point that if belief is the seed of radicalism, poverty is the fertilizer. While the reasons that radical movements spring up are complex, it is undeniable that many are drawn to these movements because they feel left out or left behind. These movements become their opportunity for justice. Beyond the necessity of developing a broadly focused antipoverty agenda, African governments must work with responsible members in the Islamic community to address any real disparities that might exist between Muslims and others in the country, particularly those who are Christian. In a number of countries, business and political leadership are dominated by Christians. This reflects the fact that Christians provided social services, from education to leadership training, as a part of their evangelizing efforts in Africa. Being better trained meant being better positioned to take advantage of opportunities after independence, be they political or business. The net effect of this is that there are real disparities between Christians and Muslims in some countries. Extremists can use these disparities as a wedge between the two groups. The strategic response to such conditions must be to create options to close the gap. One tactic not already cited might be for African governments to engage their bilateral partners in the Arab world to provide specific and direct aid through African governments to assist Muslim communities. In the same vein, governments should expand secular options to "compete" with the efforts of radical elements and fill service voids that the government might not have addressed in the past.

There also needs to be more intracontinental cooperation and coordination to identify and address the threat that such radical groups pose. As I indicated earlier, our ability to capture the terrorist in the Dar bombing was significantly enhanced by the coordination and cooperation of the Tanzanian and South African intelligence services. Africa's fight against terrorism can only be enhanced by such efforts. Correspondingly, there needs to be more intelligence gathering and sharing in cooperation with international entities and bilateral partners. A few years ago, I was asked by the then-president of the International Association of Chiefs of Police (IACP) to advise him on issues they might consider addressing. I suggested terrorism. I further suggested that they do outreach to their counterparts in Africa. Two things struck me as we explored the idea. One, the association needed to do a better job of outreach to African law enforcement officials; and two, such officials in Africa need to make a greater effort to participate in associations such as this one. To address effectively the threat of terrorism, these are precisely the types of organizations in which African law enforcement and intelligence officials need to participate.

In this article, I have outlined a number of things that need to be done to mitigate the impact of radical Islam on growth and development needs, stability, and communal needs in African countries. In a word, the strategy needs to be comprehensive. The framework for fashioning the strategic and tactical response to radical Islam must be ideological and practical, religious and rational. Kikwete's words are once again instructive relative to fashioning a framework for responding to the challenges to the radical elements in the Muslim world.

> Managing religious conflicts is perhaps one of the greatest challenges we face now, nationally and internationally. We have no choice but to work harder to promote inter- and intra-religious tolerance and understanding as we deal with religious-motivated terrorism and political violence.

The physical and ideological challenge terrorism presents for Africa is not going to go away on its own. As global pressure mounts against Muslim extremists in other areas of the world, Africa will increasingly be seen by such movements as a potential safe haven and a theater in which to attack Western interests. Muslims are found in substantial numbers in most African countries; as such, they ought to be viewed as a part of the solution to Africa's many problems, and not as the problem themselves. For Muslims to be constructively engaged in Africa's renaissance requires candid conversation about fringe elements that could threaten Africa's progress as well as clear and cogent strategies for mutual cooperation to overcome this scourge and increase Africa's potential in order to realize its promise.

Notes

1. After the August 7, 1998, attacks on the U.S. embassies in Tanzania and Kenya, retired Admiral William J. Crowe headed the Accountability Review Board charged with investigating the bombings (called the Crowe Commission). The board found the vast majority of U.S. embassies sorely lacking in their abilities to withstand transnational terrorist threats. The Crowe Commission recommended spending $14 billion over 10 years to enhance the safety of all embassies and overseas installations.

2. See The World Factbook Field Listings—Religions, available from https://www.cia.gov/library/publications/the-world-factbook/fields/2122.html?_CIA.

3. The *maitasine* are a radical Muslim element in northern Nigeria that has carried out deadly attacks on Christians in Nigeria.

4. The countries participating in this initiative are Angola, Benin, Cameroon, Equatorial Guinea, Gabon, Ghana, Nigeria, Republic of Congo, São Tomé and Principe, and Togo.

References

Adow, Mohammed. 21 July 2006. Why Ethiopia is on war footing. Available from http://news.bbc.co .uk/2/hi/5201470.stm.

Africa Confidential. 19 April 2002. Wanaharakati and Kuffar. Available from www.africa-confidential.com/ article-preview/id/527/No-Title.

Agence France Presse. 7 January 2010. Nord Mali: Paris deconseille la participation a un festival.

Chau, Donovan C. 2008. *U.S. counterterrorism in sub-Saharan Africa: Understanding costs, cultures, and conflicts.* Carlisle, PA: Strategic Studies Institute, U.S. Army War College. Available from www .strategicstudiesinstitute.army.mil/pubs/display.cfm?pubid=821.

Mamdani, Mahmood. *Good Muslim, bad Muslim*. New York, NY: Pantheon Books.

McGirk, Tim, Phil Zabriskie, Helen Gibson, Ghulam Hasnain, and Zamira Loebis. 15 September 2003. Roots of terror: Islam's other hot spots. *Time*. Available from www.time.com/time/magazine/article/0,9171,1005667,00.html (accessed 2 June 2010).

Nelson, Fred. 2007. *East Africa: Trends in coastal tourism and strategies for promoting sustainable development*. Washington, DC: Center on Ecotourism and Sustainable Development. Available from www.responsibletravel.org/resources/documents/reports/FINAL_REPORT_Fred_Nelson_Jan_08.pdf.

Radio France International. 29 December 2009. La nouvelle strategie d'AQMI en Mauritanie. Available from www.rfi.fr/contenu/20091229-aqmi-oeuvres (accessed 2 June 2010).

Solomon, Hussein. 2009. *South Africa and the fight against global terrorism*. Occasional Paper 29. Pretoria, South Africa: International Institute for Islamic Studies.

Weiser, Benjamin. 21 October 2000. Bin Laden linked to embassy blast by an ex-soldier. *New York Times*.

Debating Darfur in the World

By
ROGAIA MUSTAFA
ABUSHARAF

This article compares the debates and demonstrations about Darfur that have taken place in the Sudan, the United States, and Qatar and illuminates how political violence is apprehended and cultural identities are constructed. The rallies that occurred among Sudanese inside and outside the Sudan following the 2009 indictment of President Omar Hassan al-Bashir by the International Criminal Court (ICC) are particularly revealing. Examining what has been represented worldwide as the first genocide of the twenty-first century brings to light the ideologies that are expressed in impassioned political positions. Ideology, which implicitly undergirds the mixed emotions with which the ICC warrant was received, has been fundamental to the Darfur story from the start of the crisis in 2003. Describing Darfur in three distinct sociopolitical arenas, one sees various scenarios that are akin to a play with multiple actors and scenes, each of which is contextually mediated and expertly produced. The disconnections, ruptures, and shifts in the flow of this narration point to the disparities in the situational, local, regional, and transnational forces at work.

Keywords: Sudan; Darfur; diaspora; gender; Qatar; genocide; al-Bashir

The Sudan: Reframing Conflict

World attention focused on the Sudan following the arrest warrant issued for President Omar Hassan al-Bashir in accordance with United

NOTE: For their valuable comments on this article, I wish to thank Mark Farha, Grey Osterud, and Robert Wirsing. I am particularly appreciative of Professor Tukufu Zuberi's enthusiastic support and constructive comments and of the Sons of Greater Darfur League of Doha for their unswerving support of the project. I would also like to thank Abdel Rahman Dosa, Abdel Moniem Abu Tiffa, Shareef Harir, Mahmoud Mamdani, Gobeir Abdel Shafi, and Nazir Madibo for our extensive discussions on the predicament of Darfur. I would also like to express my gratitude to the Alexander von Humboldt Foundation and the participants of the American Philosophical Society Workshop in Berlin in November 2007. Thank you to Richard Dunn, Victoria Bernal, and Hans Peter Hans.

DOI: 10.1177/0002716210378631

Nations (UN) Security Council Resolution 1593. Acting under Chapter VII of the UN Charter, the Security Council referred the Darfur case to the prosecutor of the International Criminal Court (ICC), Luis Moreno-Ocampo. As head of state, al-Bashir was charged with five counts of crimes against humanity, including murder, extermination, forcible transfer, torture, and rape; and two counts of war crimes, for intentionally directing attacks against civilians and for pillaging.[1] During the seven years of strife in Darfur, more than 2.7 million persons have been forcibly displaced. Human rights organizations estimate the death toll at 400,000, although the government of Sudan challenged these statistics. Unfortunately, the total mortality has not been disaggregated to differentiate between deaths caused by the military and militias, those caused by displacement and other nonviolent circumstances related to the crisis, and those entirely unrelated to it. In a letter to the editor of the *Washington Post* published on May 2, 2005, Rafael Medoff of the David S. Wyman Institute for Holocaust Studies criticized the U.S. Department of State for underestimating the death toll in Darfur, just as it overestimated the number of Jewish refugees that the United States accepted during the Holocaust. Parallels between the situation in Darfur and the Holocaust have been central to the "Save Darfur" campaign, especially in the United States, where green signs saying "Not on Our Watch" remind passersby of the vow, "Never Again."

No single depiction of the Darfur crisis has managed to capture the practical and metaphorical intricacy of its representation as evocatively as the words of Yahia Adam Madibo, the *nazir* (leader) of the *Rezigat* of South Darfur: "The Darfur problem is definitely reminding us of the bad omen we attach to a crow-like flesh-eating bird named *umm kulu'lu'* (ام علك علع). When it lays its egg, everyone is forewarned: don't come near this egg because if you lift it, it will kill your mother and if you leave it alone, it will kill your father."[2] Nazir Madibo's analogy epitomizes the agonizing dilemmas facing Darfur today and suggests how the language used to describe the situation renders the crisis unsolvable. One of the thorniest predicaments with respect to the crisis in the region is the constant reiteration of ideas about the mighty Arab catching the meek African to pursue genocide or, at least, ethnic cleansing. The destruction of communities must be confronted as a complex emergency and dealt with as a matter of great urgency. Yet the deployment of the Arab versus African formulation as the sole explanatory model divorced from other sociopolitical forces shaping society in Darfur is a serious distortion. These categories did not exist in the past and are not stable in the present; they are entirely insufficient for understanding Darfurian taxonomies

Rogaia Mustafa Abusharaf, a Sudanese anthropologist, is a visiting associate professor of anthropology and culture and politics at Georgetown University's Edmund A. Walsh School of Foreign Service in Qatar. She is the author and editor of many books and articles, the most recent of which are Transforming Displaced Women *(University of Chicago Press 2009),* Female Circumcision: Multicultural Perspectives *(University of Pennsylvania Press 2006), and* Wandering: Sudanese Migrants and Exiles in North America *(Cornell University Press 2002). She was the special editor of* South Atlantic Quarterly's *winter 2010 issue, "What Is Left of the Left? The View from Sudan."*

of power and polity or even identity. Ethnological portraits painted by Sabil Yagoub, a leading Darfurian educator from Kajjar, illustrate the validity of seeing ethnological history as "a history of mixtures and movements, contacts and connections" (Razel, quoted in Probst 2007, 161). Yagoub (2005) showed that intermarriage, reciprocity, and solidarity were the ultimate organizing principles in a hybrid social formation comprising Arabs and Africans who engaged in various forms of commodity exchange and were governed by mutually recognized cultural norms and negotiated agreements. This division formed no obstacle to peaceful coexistence.[3]

The production of knowledge regarding African conditions as a whole bears out the important theoretical argument made in John Hall's *Cultures of Inquiry*: "Contemporary conflicts over knowledge have an unfortunate effect: they reinforce ideological divisions at the very time when there is an opportunity to understand the complex web of uneven connections that structure the entire range of inquiry's practices," and that "inquiry (itself) cannot be reduced to any single overarching logic" (1999, 229). When we apply Hall's approach to the question of the causes of violence in Darfur, we are prompted to critique the emphasis placed on ethnicity as the major factor in the equation. Ethnicity, as "a structure of sociability" (Jewsiewicki 2007, 136), when politically mobilized and manipulated, camouflages other fundamental dimensions of the conflict, such as banditry, land-tenure systems, land use, environmental degradation, arms proliferation and militarization, border politics, and systemic marginality. Explication of these forces is essential to any enduring settlement. To overcome the rampant oversimplification of the conflict as exclusively the product of an unbridgeable ethnic difference, we must probe history and politics, as well as culture, and trace the development of a perniciously political militancy in the region that overwhelmed previous social and economic arrangements among peoples with a history of intermixing in a complex geography.

Ladislav Holy (2006) has advanced provocative theories that challenge narratives of race as inscribed in perceptions of innate identities, indigenous or otherwise. Darfurian-Arab identities are represented as dictated by fate, rather than politics, and are not amenable to change even during processes of global transformation. The political consequences of Holy's critique are far-reaching. "The very idea of authenticity—even when thought to be used in very positive ends—had the consequence of freezing other peoples into a mythic past of homogeneous community, where, to remain authentic and thus appreciated, they could not leave" (Rapport and Overing 2007, 201). Painfully aware of the rise of militarized identities, Nazir Madibo never lost sight of the border politics involving Libya and Chad in the crisis in Darfur, even though both took measures to conceal their roles in the conflict. Drawing on decades of experiential knowledge, Madibo elucidated the politically constructed character of ethnicity, indigenity, and authenticity from within. In cataloging notions of the causes of conflict in Darfur, we find some implausible explanations: for example, Libyan leader Muammar al-Qaddafi declared to students at Cambridge University, "You may laugh to know that the root cause of the Darfur crisis was a dispute over a stolen camel" (BBC News 2007). The predominant narrative of the conflict has been one in which mostly non-Arab rebels took up arms in Darfur in early 2003, accusing the central government of neglecting their welfare, and, in response, Khartoum mobilized mostly Arab militias to subdue the insurgency. The government has also used the conflict to warn the Sudanese people of the potential negative consequences of the signing of the Comprehensive Peace Agreement in 2005 that halted the war in the south, provided for the equitable sharing of oil resources, and scheduled a referendum on independence.

In interviews that I have conducted in the Sudan since 2003, I have heard stories packed with ghastly incidents of violence that have torn apart the Sudan's social fabric. In Al-Radmmia, women spoke about the violence waged against them by both militias and bandits. In describing her forced departure, a younger Fur woman emphasized that banditry was just as dangerous to their lives as military operations, since bandits also engage in extreme brutality. The bandits' acquisition of arms from Chad was accompanied by the invention of militarized proverbs, such as *"bil klash ta'ish balash"* (شالب شيعت شالكلاب), "If you own a Kalashnikov, you can live for free." Security is jeopardized even in places not directly convulsed by violence. Given these horrific conditions, how do we recount the story of Darfur at home and to the diaspora, the arrest warrant, and the surprising responses with which the warrant was received?

When the Sudan appointed its own special prosecutor to look into reports of war crimes in Darfur, it did not lead to prosecutions, which suggests the impunity that is symptomatic of the justice institutions within the country. The president refused the ICC's persistent demand to turn over alleged war criminals, declaring unequivocally, "We will not surrender a cat to foreigners, let alone a Sudanese citizen." When the warrant for his own arrest was issued, he averred, "Judgment is not here. It is not with Ocampo or others. Our judgment is before Allah" (Sudan TV 2009).

Solidarity Rallies, Fatwas, and Chants

The ICC warrant was followed by two fatwas, or religious opinions, that were issued in a climate saturated with emotion displayed by both proponents and opponents of the indictment. These fatwas differ markedly from others that were issued in years past but not necessarily applied in Sudan. The fatwas on the ICC heightened Sudanese citizens' attention to al-Bashir's fate.

One fatwa, issued by the Higher Supreme Council of Sudanese Ulammaa (religious leaders), prohibited al-Bashir from traveling abroad for fear he would be arrested and the government would be destabilized. Al-Bashir ignored their advice, presumably to avoid losing face among the Sudanese people and other Arab nations. Al-Bashir appeared in solidarity rallies dancing, swinging his ebony cane in the air, and declaring loud and clear, "Tell Ocampo to soak his warrant and drink its water" or "Ocampo and his followers are all under my shoe" (Sudan TV 2009). Cavalier about the fatwa and the ICC, al-Bashir took several trips to

Eritrea, Qatar, Libya, and Zimbabwe; the leaders of the latter country declared that they had no obligation to surrender its controversial visitor. This response must be situated within African politics and in relation to threats from African nations to withdraw from the ICC because of its allegedly unfair treatment of Africans and Arabs. Al-Bashir, now a "fugitive from justice" in the eyes of the international community, is a bona fide hero whose personification of Arabism, Africanism, and Islamism is rolled into a single narrative of resistance to *dowal el-istikbar*, "arrogant states." Al-Bashir and his supporters contend that his powerful defiance symbolizes the end of neocolonialism.[4]

The second fatwa, certainly more controversial and potentially more consequential than its predecessor, authorized the shedding of Ocampo's blood by Islamists on the grounds that his decision represents an inexcusable assault on African and Muslim leaders who have refused to perform rituals of obedience and loyalty to the empire. A poster widely displayed in rallies in Khartoum and Darfur featured Ocampo as a pig, a symbol of filth in Muslim cosmology, and stated in bold letters, "Ocampo, you coward, al-Bashir is in the battlefield." This fatwa has been embraced and disseminated in the public domain by an alliance of organizations, "The Martyrdom Jihad Movements," which warned that it would execute suicide missions against countries championing the ICC's decision (i.e., the United States, France, and the United Kingdom). Emboldened to reveal their identities, Sudanese bloggers enumerated the members of the alliance: Supporters of Salafi Jihadists, Shihada Seekers, Banner of Martyr Shahid Abel-Fatah, League of Darfur Lions, and Nosoor Al-Bashir (Al-Bashir's Eagles). Supporters of the warrant were threatened with retribution as traitors of faith and nation. Nosoor al-Bashir was quick to abduct members of Doctors without Borders in Darfur under the pretext of protecting the country from spies masquerading as humanitarian workers.

Inflaming nationalist, Islamist, and Jihadist sentiments, Hassan Nasrallah of Hezbollah and Khalid Mishaal of Hamas embraced the view that al-Bashir was pursued for being a thorn in the empire's side because of his unyielding resistance to imperialist discourses on global security. A push for a jihad was the central theme of a long speech by Ayman al-Zawahiri, the second in command of al Qaeda, who appeared on television to ask the Sudanese to prepare themselves for a guerrilla war; al-Zawahiri invoked comparisons with situations in Iraq, Afghanistan, and Palestine. These statements for all intents and purposes evacuate the ICC of its jurisprudential legitimacy, particularly by describing its chief officer as an activist rather than a jurist and accusing him of weighing justice with two scales. Herein, it is worth noting that Sudanese history brims with nationalist passions that are linked to questions of sovereignty.[5] Sovereignty as a performance of political authority can be staged. As a solidarity rally supporter asserted, "The servant of the holy man is forced to pray."[6] A Darfurian in Doha seconded this view by describing how mobilization took place in Darfur: "If you bring people in cars you are paid a certain sum of money; you are also paid handsomely if you get people to a rally location on a horse, a donkey, or a camel."[7] In other situations, those who joined rallies cited nationhood as a reason for their decision to stand against the double standards of the international community.[8]

How do we understand the solidarity rallies that flooded the streets from Khartoum to Darfur as depicted by the Sudanese media? What were the emotional investments of those who rallied for al-Bashir? And how do we ascertain the significance of solidarity rallies in relation to public opinion under constraining circumstances? When navigating the terrain of media, we must summon Edward Herman and Noam Chomsky's *Manufacturing Consent* (2002), which offers a powerful analysis of how individuals and media organizations are prompted by political and economic forces to mold the social agenda of knowledge and belief. Media analysis helps to capture the importance of Khartoum rallies for shoring up support, whether organized or spontaneous. Rallies of solidarity for al-Bashir elevated morale to new heights and gave al-Bashir the confidence to promise to track down war criminals in Darfur in a speech addressing a crowd of thousands in Zalingei, one of the most politically charged towns in Darfur (Hamdi 2009). I followed Sudan TV's daily news program *What They Are Saying about the So-Called ICC* (2009), which broadcasts within and outside of the Sudan the protest demonstrations across the Sudan. Skeptics argue that under political dictatorships, public opinion cannot be measured by massive demonstrations. Not only has the extent of political mobilization in favor of al-Bashir been unprecedented, but it also offers an illustrative example of the theatrical performance of sovereignty and resistance to neocolonialism.

In the Sons of Southern States Solidarity Rally, al-Bashir appeared in a feathered headdress, leopard-skin skirt, ox horns, beads, and amulets. Chants of "Hallelujah" and "Allah Akbar" were transmitted by huge speakers in the yard of Saddaqqa Hall by the River Nile. Millions of southerners in Khartoum vowed that they were willing to die for the Sudan, if al-Bashir were targeted. Southern leaders, sultans, and politicians voiced their solidarity with a "man who brought peace to the south" and concluded the six-hour event by taking a solemn oath to stand by him. Accounts from southerners in Khartoum have drawn attention to the complicated political dynamics that have pervaded the Sudan. For example, major Darfurian leaders, such as Khalil Ibrahim of the Justice and Equality Movement (JEM), were key players in the Sudanese "holy war" in the south among a regiment "Dababbeen," and Darfurian jihadists were part and parcel of the assault against so-called infidels. A southern Darfurian explained this situation plainly: "We spared no effort to offer our lives in sacrifice for jihad in the path of Allah. We were at the frontlines in the war in southern Sudan. When the Islamists recruited us, we obliged. The majority of those who joined jihad in southern Sudan did so of their own volition. In fact, we revered the cause and the people like Sheikh Hassan Al-Turabi. At one point if he asked us to pray west, we would have gladly prayed west."[9]

At a sizable rally in southern Darfur that was featured on Sudan TV (2009), al-Bashir shifted responsibility for the Darfur crisis to the supernatural world: "Curse the Satan who got into your midst and wreaked havoc? Brothers, it is Satan who pushed you to do what you have done to one another. Curse him, curse him." After designating Satan as the responsible party for the cataclysm, al-Bashir proceeded to explain the conspiracy of imperialism to conquer the Sudan through the gateway of Darfur. A Sudanese TV correspondent reported that "there was no obvious sign of opposition at the rally where Bashir arrived on the back of an open truck, as streams of white-robed Darfuris rode past him on horses and camels. On the edges of the crowd, people climbed trees and stood on the raised scoop of an industrial digger to get a better view" (Sudan TV 2009). Considering these responses, political leaders in opposition parties who stood by al-Bashir noted that whether people have rallied in support of al-Bashir is quite peripheral under interventionist pretexts. To assert that rallies of solidarity indicate Sudanese rejection of the ICC is insufficient, since their strong links to nationalist passions and questions of sovereignty must be brought to bear upon what is largely perceived as a neocolonial confrontation. Worldwide, rallies drew thousands of demonstrators who echoed these sentiments by denouncing the double standard of international law and enunciated their reproof of the ICC. A few Darfurians departed from this position by remonstrating against any possible intervention and siding with selective and compartmentalized justice. These responses, whether in support of or opposition to the ICC, cannot be treated as homogeneous political actions.

Racializing and Feminizing Darfur in Diasporic Politics

How do we decode the responses of the Sudanese who backed the warrant, and what comparative political lessons can we extract from the support it found in the United States? Before describing how and why rallies in response to the ICC's warrant varied, we need to understand the fundamental principles of the Darfurian diaspora. Two major, interlinked constructs of racialization and feminization have been central to the representation of the conflict as one in which Arab janjaweed militias have annihilated Africans in a proxy war using rape as a characteristic tactic. In the vocabulary of the Darfur conflict, *janjaweed* means Arab. As several observers have pointed out, these "devils on horseback" actually consist of many different groups, including bandits, militias, and mercenaries from Senegal, Chad, Mali, and Libya. Nevertheless, incidents of rape of indigenous women by the janjaweed have turned centrally on race.

To understand how race and gender converged in American thinking, we draw on African and African-American scholars' perspectives on diasporas, particularly the question of how communities form in relation to migration and home. According to historian Paul Zeleza, whose work explores the relevance of diaspora to concepts of time and place, "Diaspora—refers to a process, a condition, a space, and a discourse, the continuous process by which a diaspora is made, unmade and remade, the changing conditions in which it lives and expresses itself, the place where it is molded and imagined, and the contentious ways in which it is studied and discussed" (2007, 87). Probing how diasporas are made, Matory asks "why certain rubrics and visions of community appear to prevail over others at a given moment in a given place" and answers, "Any given imagination of community will favor strategic interests over others" (2005, 89). I contend that strategic interests are organic to Darfurian involvement in sculpting the politics of advocacy vis-à-vis their homeland, despite that these interests are often circumscribed and curtailed by how new associations with Jewish and Christian faith-based organizations are viewed by devout Muslim Darfurians whose identities supersede their ethnicities. Responding to a call to join "communities of conscience" consisting of interfaith groups, Darfurians in the United States have forged strategic alliances that are deeply at odds with Darfurians at home, both in the forms of activism that they adopt and in their consciousnesses about who they are. Although some common denominators galvanize Darfurian communities to campaign for change, the diaspora experience in the United States is different, both existentially and ontologically. Agitation for political representation, reducing indices of marginalization, and enforcement of accountability all have been advocated in migrant and home communities alike. However, disentangling the responses to the ICC of the Darfurian diaspora in the United States uncovers a spectacular metamorphosis of their identities through amalgamating into formations that James Clifford (1994, 311) describes as "racialized sojourns."

The issuance of the arrest warrant was followed by rallies supporting the ICC in cities such as Boston, New York, Washington, and San Diego. However, these events differed sharply from their counterparts in the Sudan and other countries. The rallies in the United States celebrated the chief prosecutor for making a decision that was thought to be a decisive victory for the sullied, a welcome reprieve to the debased populace of Darfur. This response evinced a shift in subject positions that necessitates deeper epistemological explication of Darfurians' acquisition of a black identity in North America. In terms of both geography and history, Darfur is part and parcel of the largely Arabized northern Sudan. Arabic is the lingua franca, despite the presence of numerous local languages (i.e., Fur, Masalit, Zhagawa, Dajo, Siniar, Bargood, Barno, Fellata, Um Bararro, and Maidoob). As to "the complexion of race" before the crisis, blackness—or *zurga*, which literally means not blackness but blueness—was not in and of itself a reason for differentiation and ethnic tension (see Wheeler 2000). Alterity did not prompt massacres. Within local notions of the political sociology of pigmentation, Arabs and zurga intermarried and coexisted peacefully. When disputes erupted, they were swiftly resolved through locally based justice institutions. Visitors observed that they could not tell Arabs and non-Arabs apart. In 1932, the Seligmans noted, "We could not on our brief visit discover any language other than Arabic, but this is far from conclusive as everyone was anxious to impress us with their Arab and Islamic affinities" (1932, 448). "Darfurian" as an idiomatic term for a singular identity did not exist in the Sudanese vocabulary prior to the conflict in Darfur. This term is a foreign designation born out of specific patterns of representation and cultural production around a people who previously viewed themselves as Afro-Arabs and Sudanese citizens. Darfurian now signifies a newly assigned black identity as opposed to a homogenized Arab janjaweed. These shifts cannot be understood in isolation of the specific context in which Darfurians craft their selves as black, de-Arabized victims. Race holds the master status in America; skin color supersedes all other markers of ethno-cultural identity.

My ethnographic observations at Darfur-related conferences, rallies, meetings, and town hall events on college campuses testify to radically different discourses on political and cultural identities in comparison to that among Darfurians in the Sudan and among those Darfurians in exile in the Gulf. If Peter Probst had the opportunity to comment on this entangled situation in relation to African modernities, ethnographic imaginations, and the interwovenness of ideas in cultural realities, he might argue, "In this highly dynamic milieu of contacts and connections, diffusionism was seen to be a kind of cultural geology which attempted to order the surface chaos resulting out of the overall cultural mixture by sorting out its various elements according to the historical sequence by which the different cultural 'flows' had crossed one another" (Probst 2007, 163–64). Darfur's morphology can be understood from this perspective.

In the United States, a steady process of racializing Darfur has been set into motion. We must ponder the cumulative effect of this burgeoning racialization that has come from testimonies from academics who are producing anthologies on Darfur without the presence of a single Darfurian voice—which provides ample demonstration of exclusionary practices—to others whose work is geared toward public audiences, such as Brian Steidle, a former captain in the Marine Corps who served in Darfur. The jacket of his 2007 book, *The Devil Came on Horseback: Bearing Witness to the Genocide in Darfur*, reads, "Day after day Brian watched a 'Janjaweed' (devil on a horse) and Government of Sudan troops attack not just Darfurian rebel groups, but black African civilians." In New York City, Washington, D.C., and Bloomington—the latter has been the main U.S. abode of Darfurians recently—the Darfurian diaspora has been surrounded by a deep sense of sorrow and sympathy as a vanishing people, an identify bestowed upon them by celebrities garnering tremendous influence to urge their representatives in the U.S. government to keep the pressure on the Sudanese government. This call was repeated on numerous occasions: an art exhibit put together by a Worcester African festival that called for more rallies and demonstrations; national speaking tours by figures such as Daoud Hari,[10] who was arrested in Chad but released through the mediation of New Mexico governor Bill Richardson; and petitions to elected representatives. How did this disapora come into being, and how do we apprehend their views on sovereignty since they are by far the most ardent supporters of intervention? Have Darfurians in the disapora suspended sovereignty and eschewed dialogue on reconciliation? Darfurians in the Sudan and Qatar think these new community formations are potentially useful in attracting media attention. This momentous responsibility notwithstanding, they are by and large redefining themselves and tactically reassessing what it means to belong in America.

Diasporic politics and ideologies as expressed in rallies and events in the United States have had long gestations and lack the spontaneity of their counterparts in Khartoum. These rallies mobilized the language of victimization as the main medium for telling the world about the brutality sweeping a region "the size of France." Although this notion of spontaneity ought to be approached with a measure of skepticism, it figures prominently in comparisons drawn between home and exile modes of organizing actions of accommodation and protest. Before proceeding further, however, we must contextualize the diaspora to elucidate the series of events that led to their unwavering support of President George W. Bush's policy in the Sudan. In the large scheme of things, Bush's policy linked an African story as told in the world's sole superpower to a political economy of pity in which visits by Angelina Jolie and George Clooney and charity parties in Central Park made engagement with Darfur an entirely different enterprise.

As far as self-aggrandizement is concerned, Darfurians are no different from other diasporic communities, such as those well described in Paul Hockenos's *Homeland Calling: Exile and Patriotism and the Balkan Wars* (2003), Orville Schell's *Virtual Tibet: Searching for Shangri-La from the Himalayas to Hollywood* (2000), and Robert Levine's *Cuban Miami* (2000). As numerous ethnographic examples demonstrate, diasporas have a tremendous weight on the formulation of foreign policy vis-à-vis homelands. I share Robert Wirsing's concerns about the concept of the strategic potential of ethnic diasporas (2007, 19); for although he acknowledges the considerable difficulties in mobilizing diasporas on the basis of historical lessons drawn from the notion of Nazi Germany's "Fifth Column," he raises poignant points about the nature of political mobilization and manipulation of ethnic minorities that bear striking current resemblance to the Darfurian diaspora. My concurrence with Wirsing in delineating the distortion and misappropriation of diasporic power rests on the doubts of displaced Darfurians inside the Sudan and their utter aversion to an activism they depict as "opportunistic hotel opposition."[11] Citing the presence of JEM leaders in England and Sudanese Liberation Movement (SLM) leaders in Paris as illustrative examples, Darfurians ask, "What does activism and roaming the world from hotel to hotel mean for our suffering people in Kalma?"[12] Who has the right to represent Darfur is a question that lies at the heart of the unmistakable lack of enthusiasm that those struggling at home display whenever the U.S. diaspora is discussed.

The idea that overseas activism represents a new commerce of war can be gleaned from the accounts of those who never left the Sudan, whether by choice or through lack of opportunity. In Al Azhari Park in Al-Shuhhadda, Omdurman, I had extensive conversations with members of a rather small-scale Darfurian nongovernmental organization (NGO) working with displaced people. The challenges faced by these smaller NGOs are enormous, as they have meager resources and must compete for funding with larger, more established organizations. When I asked about their familiarity with international NGOs and interfaith coalitions, such as Save Darfur, that are raising funds through activities arranged by Hollywood celebrities and smaller ones such as selling green plastic bracelets and T-shirts that say "Save Darfur," they responded,

> We have neither heard of them, nor of the green plastic bracelets they are selling. No one is helping and we have to fend for ourselves as we always did. Activism inside the Sudan requires a lot of courage and innovation. We don't have access to technology and the internet here costs large amounts of money. Victims of war and displacement in the Sudan have no means of expressing or complaining about their problems or engaging in any of the activities that those abroad undertake. Most of them lack knowledge of the

law, and even we have to say that it is not always on their side. Illiteracy plagues so many of our people and of courses this affects how they frame their complaints. There are so many NGOs in Darfur who only use satellite images but do not necessarily listen to the voices of the innocent people who are hurt deeply by people telling stories on their behalf. Individuals who do that have no credibility and they are unwilling to get their information from the source, from the people who have so much to say.[13]

In light of these widely held reservations, this diaspora is seen largely as a liability rather than an asset to the cause since their activism has awarded them benefits they would have not have enjoyed had they chosen other paths of resistance.

On another occasion, a member of one of the armed movements in Darfur remarked, "*nas el mihjar*, the people in diaspora, especially the opposition leaders who are refusing our call for collective action of unification, are benefiting from the backing of international organizations. They are gaining weight and their skin is glowing. They have no idea of what we experience in the field but they still want to come back to govern."[14] These statements dovetail Mahmood Mamdani's critique of Save Darfur in *Saviors and Survivors: Darfur, Politics, and the War on Terror* (2009), in which he dissects the movement's methods of the advertisement and commodification of suffering. While Sudanese at home rallied because of political pressure to "perform" sovereignty, the Darfurian diaspora in the United States were also subject to systematic political mobilization by Save Darfur.

Various host societies provide a range of opportunities for what can or cannot be narrated. The fact that victimhood came into view as a building block in the project of racialized identities provides ample testament to the particular spaces, resources, and alliances made available to Darfurians in the United States. The Omdurman interviewee is correct to point out that cyber-power is breaking new ground and producing radical changes in political practice and participation. It creates virtual internet nations over which no one can exercise unlimited control. Viewers are invited to zoom in to see the destruction of Darfurian villages and to call or e-mail the White House. By virtue of Google Earth technology, Darfur is counted alongside Auschwitz, Warsaw, and other sites of untold suffering. Other diasporas have also been transformed by the internet; Hockenos (2003) has written compellingly about how the explosion of transnational phenomena, from Web sites to multinational corporations, facilitates the business of Balkan diasporas. Linking up with some of the most powerful voices in American circles, Darfurians were in the forefront of supporting Senator Richard Durbin's legislation on foreign corporations' divestment (Sudan Accountability and Divestment Act 2007). When recounting a fraction of a huge movement that contains hundreds of organizations, Darfurian articulation of their rerouted identities (see Clifford 1994) becomes increasingly significant both theoretically and methodologically as community becomes linked to global politics while affording the opportunity to compare ruptures between these identities and those who never left the besieged region.

These collaborative efforts have not only contributed to shaping foreign policy vis-à-vis Darfur but have also produced international discourses about the region by crafting public opinion in ways that reinforce the oversimplification

that commonly occurs in African affairs at the global level (see Grzyb 2009).
Theoretically, an understanding of Darfurian diasporic discourses in the United
States points to significant differences between the diaspora and their counterparts in the Sudan and Qatar, especially the emphasis that Darfurians in the
United States put on narratives of race. The shift from being part of the Sudan's
so-called Arab North to being black Africans par excellence illuminates shifting
strategic interests in the shaping of a diasporic community's political representation of what has been designated as the African Holocaust.[15]

Darfur in the feminine

Elsewhere, I formulated a thesis of competing masculinities that convert
women's bodies as primary targets for men to settle the scores among one
another under circumstances of extreme political violence (Abusharaf 2006a).
The feminization of Darfur through narratives of victimization and suffering that
paint the region as a violated female body became the dominant story in a region
whose affliction became synonymous with the cruel and inhumane treatment of
women. In situations of political conflicts, women and girls indeed suffer violence
disproportionately in comparison to males. Discourses on moral responsibility and
humanitarian rescue have figured centrally in debating international responses to
these horrors, which were described as systematic tools of forced migration and
ethnic cleansing. Influential journalists such as Nicholas D. Kristof (2005)
pointed to the existence of "A Policy of Rape." In societies without the most basic
structures of democracy and observance of human rights, these violent acts have
horrible implications for the women involved. Rape has featured predominantly
in the activism of the U.S. diasporic community; rape and racialization have gone
hand in hand.

I recall a particularly painful occasion when Darfurian victimization was put on
display. A group of female peace activists were asked to join a Darfurian family in
Alexandria, Virginia, for a dinner party (of which I was a part). Upon arrival, we
were warmly welcomed and introduced to a large number of Darfurian guests.
Our host called upon his young daughter, a child of no more than seven years old,
to greet us and tell the story of Darfur and the janjaweed. The child was very
clearly ill at ease but yielded: "The janjaweed are bad Arab people. They attack
black women in Darfur. They do bad things, steal their belongings, and torture
them. They even threw babies in the fire." The father, filled with pride at his
child's recitation of the gruesome acts of violence and barbarity, led a round of
applause for her. This striking incident illustrates the pattern of community formation in the United States and underlines how women are becoming the quintes-
sential victims in new imaginings of a region far away. Rape, as a means of
genocide, invokes emotions and racializes Darfurian identities, as annihilation of
a race is carried out through impregnation of blacks by Arabs.

In Darfur, we must also take into consideration reports such as Amnesty
International's "Sudan: Darfur: Rape as a Weapon of War." The report includes
an eyewitness account of *hakamat* (حكامات), "female traditional singers," who

congratulated men for sexual assaults perpetrated against other women: "The blood of the Blacks runs like water, we take their goods and we chase them from our area and our cattle will be in their land. The power of al-Bashir belongs to the Arabs and we will kill you until the end, you Blacks, we have killed your God" (Amnesty International 2004). These reports, though discredited, found their way into the stories of émigrés embracing new narratives about "black" people murdered by light-skinned Arabs.[16] Impregnating women with "light-skinned babies" has pervaded the reporting on rape in Darfur, casting the conflict in terms of black versus Arab. Witness these tendencies in the statement by a female refugee from a Masalit village who was interviewed by Amnesty International in Goz Amir in Chad (2004): "I was sleeping when the attack on Disa started. I was taken away by the attackers [who] were all in uniforms. They took dozens of other girls and made us walk. . . . During the day we were beaten and they were telling us: 'You black we will exterminate you, you have no god.' At night we were raped several times. [They] guarded us with arms and we were not given food for three days." A Darfurian residing in Doha refuted this story; no one would tell Darfurians they have no god, for they are known throughout Africa as pious Muslims, bearers of the Quran.

The weaponization of sex has been a priority for African-Americans at FinalCall. com, a Web site that suggests that the United States and the United Kingdom are causing and then exaggerating a "crisis" in the Sudan. President al-Bashir appeared on FinalCall.com in a live, interactive satellite video conference with members of the Nation of Islam and reporters attending the 2007 Saviors' Day conference in Detroit, Michigan. African-Americans in Detroit were keenly interested in asking their questions about ethnic cleansing directly to President al-Bashir. The president critiqued the terms in which the conflict had been presented: "Talk of Arabs killing blacks is a lie. The government of Sudan is a government of blacks, with all different ethnic backgrounds. We are all Africans, we are all blacks" (Muhammad 2007, 1). Impregnating black women with light-skinned babies seems unimaginable when the Sudan is seen as "the Land of the Blacks."[17]

When Darfur Arrived in Doha

The state of Qatar has been a fascinating locality from which to compare organized political activism around Darfur, with respect to migration and the diaspora from Darfur, and the race of Darfurians. Qatar is host to one of the largest civic groups of Sudanese overseas, especially in the countries of the Gulf Cooperation Council, which comprises thousands of migrants from assorted ethnic and occupational backgrounds, including a large number of Darfurians. Here, neither racialization nor feminization figure as they did in diasporic communities in the United States. Indeed, Darfurian intellectuals in Doha resist ethnicization. Although fully cognizant of the intermingling of ethnicity and politics, a Darfurian migrant made it clear that the group had made a deliberate decision to identify itself as part of the Sons of Greater Darfur League. The group worked painstakingly to deconstruct the perceived homogenized Arab response toward the violence inflicted upon Africans. Darfurians in Doha testify to the pervasive violence, but they situate it within the deeper conflicts that afflict the region as a whole. Similar to other civic groups that adhere to the slogans of nationalism, their support is not for al-Bashir but for the nation. As a lawyer put it, the "al-Bashir government is an oppressive dictatorship that does not represent the Sudanese people. It does not work on our behalf, but still that does not mean that an outside and imposed solution will be the answer" (Sudan TV 2009). Some Sudanese, including Darfurians, joined solidarity rallies justifying their support by their overwhelming concern about foreign policies that have failed elsewhere.

Qatar has been the foremost political stage on which diplomacy has focused on reconstituting goodwill among the "segmentary lineages" pervading Darfurian politics today. The government has extraordinary vision, and the country is wealthy and cosmopolitan, with hypermodernity standing alongside tradition. With its discernible weight in world affairs, Doha is constructing the infrastructure for peace in the Sudan, with strong backing from the parties involved. Sudanese migrants attest to the fact that the intersecting agendas of states and nonstate actors that had permeated the prominent political discourse in their war-torn society do not exist in Doha. Prepared to renounce the discourse of victimization, Darfurians in Doha exhibit greater commitment to deal with the problematic native politics; the prospects of reconciliation; citizenship; Darfurian-Darfurian dynamics; banditry; border disputes; water, land, and the environment; and Islamism. Dealing with these difficult predicaments is solidified by Qatar's engagement in the tragedy, not only at the levels of its foreign policy and diplomatic priorities but also at the level of Qatari and Sudanese civil societies. Qatari civil society has assumed a key role in connecting with large segments of the Sudanese in Doha and Darfur. The Qatari Red Crescent, in concert with local branches that it has established in Darfur, has designated Darfur as an utmost priority. It has consolidated its links with the Sudanese Women's League, as part of the Higher Popular Committee for Darfur's Peace; the former, in cooperation with Qatari citizens, has been instrumental in various aid and rehabilitation assistance programs for Darfur.

Dialogues around social peace have grown to be the characteristic marker of Darfurian activism in Doha, without ignoring the principal causes of the crisis. In Doha, activists have abundant opportunities to contribute to presentations, focus groups, peace initiatives, debates,[18] and interviews with key players in Darfurian politics, ranging from lunch with representatives of JEM, teaching courses on public anthropology to Qatari students, attending Red Crescent events held in collaboration with the Sudanese Women's League, and talking to leaders of armed factions who arrived at Doha in search of reunification to interviewing the first Darfurian to surrender himself to The Hague. As my interests in diasporic politics expanded to incorporate multiple sites of inquiry about migrants' and exiles' political lives, Darfurians in Doha offered me a unique opportunity to examine members of a political society who had previously been regarded as economic migrants, who had been pushed by dire circumstances at home and lured by financial rewards abroad.

Rakoobat Ajaweed Darfur (روفراد ديواجا ةبوكار)

One of the most noticeable efforts in Doha from which the Darfurian diaspora draws inspiration is a forum founded by the Arab Democracy Foundation called "Rakoobat Ajaweed Darfur." The Rakoobat is a reconciliatory forum and is led by revered elders and native chiefs who once wielded enormous moral authority in native government. The leaders used to gather and bring perpetrators, bandits, and criminals to justice after days of deliberations. In many ways it is an embodiment of civil society, and its vision has been deeply rooted in restoring peace and tranquility. The son of a former Maalia chief remarked in Doha, a "Long time ago when bandits ran havoc in our community, my father would send people to capture and bring them to him. He worked in counsel with other chiefs and took necessary measures for bringing the stolen animals back. Our native leaders followed all the principles of transitional justice talked about today. No one who is not familiar with the power of native leaders could appreciate the magnitude of loss that our region endured as a result of their marginalization" (Arab Democracy Foundation Workshop 2009). In an inaugural event, Mohsen Marzug, Rakoobat's director, remarked that the efforts of the Rakoobat are designed to reintegrate the opinions of native leaders in the process of establishing local peace. "Today is one of these moments that enable individuals and communities to make history for themselves and for those who come after them. This moment alone is capable to aid us in circumventing crisis, otherwise irresolvable by weaponry or illusions of grandeur" (Arab Democracy Foundation Workshop 2009). Darfurian migrants and members from the Sudan discuss their aspirations in this forum to take advantage of experiments in social peace and other mechanisms for cementing transitional justice. Involving victims, regardless of their role in interethnic violence, leaders craft pragmatic steps toward moral and material reparations. These steps toward peaceful coexistence aim to remedy the security deficits that emerged as an outcome of the deliberate weakening of native leaders, addressing gender-based violence regardless of who committed the act, such as rapes. The forum has drawn inspiration from the formidable Moroccan Truth Commission jurist, Ahmed Shawqi Baniob, who declared that "we all have to bid the victims within us farewell if we are to move forward, restore trust, and support a culture of peace" (Arab Democracy Foundation Workshop 2009).

Sufism

Another extraordinary initiative for promoting social peace in Darfur has emanated from the passionate philosophy of Sufism. Working hand in glove with native leaders who once wielded considerable moral authority has helped the Sufists to lay out the spiritual underpinnings of their declaration. Sufi pillar Sheikh Musa Abdallah Hussein's efforts follow along the lines sketched by Sheikh Ibrahim Salih Al-Hussein, the grand mufti of Nigeria, who has a substantial number of disciples in Darfur. The Sufi call began in 2007, starting in Al-Fashir, Al-Geinana, and Nyala, where more than 10,000 cassette tapes were distributed to spread the word about Sufism. Sufism's focus on reconciliation was consolidated in a vision of peace that addresses matters lying at the basis of Darfur's social structure. Indeed, so unyielding was the Sufi message that many Salfi (fundamentalists) found themselves in awe of its influential and benevolent mode of conflict resolution. Sufism's philosophical perspective does not differentiate on the basis of hierarchy but reorients its energy to define reconciliatory practices at the levels of villages, states, and border countries. Emancipating individuals' thinking from a fixation on vengeance, addressing existential problems, and returning to native governance are messages that have enjoyed enormous respect in Doha. Sufism's denunciation of ethnic hatred and racial supremacy has met a positive response from Darfurians of every ethnic origin in Qatar.

While the Darfurian diaspora in the United States has made it clear through Save Darfur that accountability for al-Bashir tops its agenda, their counterparts in Doha have found it imperative to engage multiple actors in dialogue around key strategic issues, including improvement of the conditions of the displaced and forced migrants so as to guarantee relief operations without hindrances and impediments, release and exchange of prisoners, reduction of violence and ending atrocities within three months, and the establishment of a framework for the peace process. Darfurian intellectuals are grappling with many issues to ensure inclusiveness in ways that set them apart from the U.S. diaspora. According to a Darfurian in Doha, "A call for a Darfurian-Darfurian dialogue [has been] rendered as the most critical piece in the puzzle. Peace negotiations must be built on [a] strong base of popular support by parties representing the entire spectrum of the Sudanese political rainbow" (Arab Democracy Foundation Workshop 2009). Concerned citizens, as well as other armed factions, are only averse to acknowledging statements by Khalil Ibrahim of the JEM, who is not only at war with other segments of Darfur's insurgents but has promised to crush everyone on his path and claimed that no other rebel movement in Darfur enjoys power or legitimacy.

Darfurians in Doha consider Darfur a problem that does not warrant the compartmentalization that arises from asking such questions as whether the crisis is an ethnic or a national one. One Doha migrant notes, "Unless we look at Darfur as part of a larger national scene we will fall in the trap of failed agreements that were beleaguered by dual modalities and dismiss the legitimacy of numerous forces of resistance on the ground."[19] The Darfurian diaspora's approach in Doha is profoundly at odds with its American counterpart. It rallies behind reparation and reconciliation and protests language that fuels hatred and vengeance. These views were rendered with crystal clarity when migrants organized a gathering with Abu Garda, the first to surrender himself to The Hague, and with the various factions of armed forces who came to Doha in search of unity in diversity.

Conclusion

While recognizing the subjectivity and agency of Darfurians at home and in the diaspora in crafting peace, it behooves Sudanese people to create dialogues to remedy their shattered communities. Spaces must be carved out that place the production of knowledge, thought, and representation back in the location where they matter the most: in Darfur and the Sudan. Being a pawn in other people's designs, as Ali Mazrui puts it, has helped to weave stories about Darfur that are of a very different character. In the midst of passions, pity, propaganda, and polarization, debating Darfur requires a special objectivity and distance from approaches that enlarge the rifts and fragmentation that keep the tragedy going and halt efforts to effect sustainable peace in a society under siege.

Notes

1. Chief Prosecutor Ocampo had filed genocide charges against President al-Bashir the previous year, and the ICC did not rule out bringing genocide charges in the future.

2. Interview with Nazir Madibo, Doha, Qatar, April 2009.

3. The negotiations that had previously facilitated the sharing of resources between groups resulted from President Jaafar Nimeiri's policy of undermining local justice administration, especially native chiefs, in a situation of environmental stress, coupled with the introduction of weapons and the involvement of Chad.

4. Reading this response within the political moment invites a rethinking of the relevance of Pan-African and Pan-Arab nationalisms, which are both in a state of flux. Unbeknownst to al-Bashir, incorporating *dowal el-istikbar* in the Sudanese political lexicon revives, albeit inadvertently, an argument advanced by Lenin at the Second Comintern Congress: "The world consists of oppressing and oppressed nations (not only classes); the former are a small minority; the latter, a huge majority" (quoted in Filatova 2007, 204). Invocations of sovereignty in the current political mobilization are understandable; even the United States does not recognize the ICC's jurisdiction because it represents an infringement on national sovereignty.

5. The epistemological and philosophical roots of the idea of sovereignty cannot be explored here (see Hoffman 1998; Jackson 2003); neither can the fascinating notion of sovereignty as "organized hypocrisy" (Krasner 1999). In exploring the relevance of sovereignty, I rely on observations and interviews following Sudanese and non-Sudanese television coverage of the verdict.

6. Personal communication, 2009.

7. Personal communication, Sons of Greater Darfur League, 2009.

8. I suggest that sovereignty is relational or a relative rather than an absolute form of thought; it can and cannot be feigned in particular situations; it is contingent and politically constructed, rather than carved in stone. Sovereignty in the Sudanese context at home and abroad is intricately woven in discourses on nation, home, and belonging. The negative responses to the warrant raise questions regarding the role of nationalist emotions and the paramount significance of collective rage. The political subjectivity and agency of those who participated in solidarity rallies worldwide from Khartoum to Kuala Lumpur, and those who decided not to join, cannot be interpreted in functionalist terms. Instead, I consider this situation an open-ended field of patterns and processes that merit investigation. Elsewhere (Abusharaf 2006b), I described an incident of anticolonial protest in late 1940s British Sudan relying on Jean-Paul Sartre's explication of the phenomenology of emotions linked to structures of consciousness (1948, 15). Some elements from the phenomenological constructivist approach not only further our understanding of sociopolitical values as lived but also help to frame an important question with respect to the discourses of nationhood in world politics.

9. Personal communication, 2009.

10. Hari is a Darfurian who was arrested in 2006, along with a reporter for whom he was working as a translator in Chad and the Sudan. Hari's book, *The Translator: A Tribesman's Memoir of Darfur* (2008), recounts his arrest and what unfolded thereafter.

11. "Hotel opposition" is a widely used term that reflects the sentiment among Sudanese in the Sudan that the diaspora is benefiting from the conflict in the Sudan.

12. Personal communication with a Darfurian, Al Azhari Park, Omdurman, Sudan, December 2007.

13. Ibid.

14. Personal communication with a Darfurian, Doha, April 2009.

15. Since writing *Wanderings: Sudanese Migrants and Exiles in North America* (Abusharaf 2002), I have noted the presence of Darfurians in the United States, most of whom are not newcomers to America as are refugees from south Sudan. Even when looked upon as a black Darfurian diaspora, they are not homogeneous; and political differences among Masalit, Fur, and Zaghwa in the United States are sharpened by ethnicization.

16. This theme is reiterated in a large amount of literature on rape as a weapon of war, including reports of NGOs and personal autobiographies written by Darfurians with the assistance of professional writers. Halima Bashir, the physician who coauthored *Tears of the Desert* (2008) attesting to atrocities against women in Darfur, has returned to the Sudan since the publication of her testimony and now holds a government post.

17. Throughout history, travelers have translated "Sudan" as "Land of the Blacks".

18. On April 27, 2009, the Qatar Foundation and BBC World allocated their Doha Debates to Darfur by posing a proposition: "This House believes that Arab states should hand over the Sudanese president to the International Criminal Court." Moderated by the formidable Tim Sebastian, founder and chairman of the Doha Debates and recipient of most prestigious Royal Television Society's Interviewer of the Year Award, the forum was a heated discussion between those speaking for the motion, including Hani Shukralla (former chief editor of the Egypt-based *Al-Ahram* weekly) and Ahmed Hussein Adam (Justice and Equality Movement spokesman) and those against the motion, including Ghazi Salahuddin Alatabani (Sudanese advisor to al-Bashir and on the Darfur Portfolio) and Ronald Marchal (senior research fellow at CNRS, Paris, and former editor of *Politique Africaine*). The house voted for the motion, but only by a small majority. See Doha Debates (2009).

19. Personal discussions, Doha, Qatar, 2009.

References

Abusharaf, Rogaia Mustafa. 2002. *Wanderings: Sudanese migrants and exiles in North America*. Ithaca, NY: Cornell University Press.

Abusharaf, Rogaia Mustafa. 2006a. Competing masculinities: Probing political disputes as acts of violence against women in southern Sudan and Darfur. *Human Rights Review* 7 (2): 59–75.

Abusharaf, Rogaia Mustafa. 2006b. "We Have Supped So Deep in Horrors": Understanding colonialist emotionality and British responses to female circumcision in northern Sudan. *History & Anthropology* 3:209–28.

Amnesty International. 2004. Sudan: Darfur: Rape as a weapon of war: Sexual violence and its consequences. AFR 54/076/04. London: Amnesty International. Available from www.amnesty.org/en/library/asset/AFR54/076/2004/en/f66115ea-d5b4-11dd-bb24-1fb85fe8fa05/afr540762004en.pdf (accessed 15 June 2010).

Arab Democracy Foundation Workshop on Civic Peace and Transitional Justice in Darfur. 2009. 30 March–3 April. Doha, Qatar.

Bashir, Halima. 2008. *Tears of the desert: A memoir of survival in Darfur*. With Damien Lewis. New York, NY: One World Ballantine Books.

BBC News. 23 October 2007. Darfur "a quarrel over a camel." Available from http://news.bbc.co.uk (accessed 30 April 2009).

Clifford, James. 1994. Diasporas. *Cultural anthropology* 9 (3): 302–38.

Doha Debates. 27 April 2009. This House believes that Arab states should hand over the Sudanese president to the International Criminal Court. Available from www.thedohadebates.com/debates/debate.asp?d=49&s=5&mode=speakers (accessed 8 June 2010).

Filatova, Irina. 2007. Anti-colonialism in Soviet African Studies (1920–1960). In *The study of Africa: Global and transnational engagments*, ed. Paul Tiyambe Zeleza, vol. 2, 203–35. Dakar, Senegal: Council for the Development of Social Science Research in Africa.

Grzyb, Amanda. 2009. *The world and Darfur: International response to crimes against humanity in western Sudan*. Montreal, Canada: McGill-Queens University Press.

Hall, John. 1999. *Cultures of inquiry: From epistemology to discourse in sociohistorical research*. Cambridge, UK: Cambridge University Press.

Hamdi, Ibrahim. 7 April 2009. Sudan's Bashir vows to try darfur war criminals. Reuters. Available from www.reuters.com/article/idUSL718741.

Hari, Daoud. 2008. *The translator: A tribesman's memoir of Darfur*. New York, NY: Random House.

Herman, Edward, and Noam Chomsky. 2002. *Manufacturing consent: The political economy of the mass media*. New York, NY: Pantheon Books.

Hockenos, Paul. 2003. *Homeland calling: Exile patriotism and the Balkan Wars*. Ithaca, NY: Cornell University Press.

Hoffman, John. 1998. *Sovereignty: Concepts in social thought in the social sciences*. Minneapolis, MN: University of Minnesota Press.

Holy, Ladislav. 2006. *Religion and custom in a Muslim society: The Berti of Sudan*. Cambridge, UK: Cambridge University Press.

Jackson, John. 2003. Sovereignty-Modern: A new approach to an outstanding concept. *American Journal of International Law* 97:782–802.

Jewsiewicki, Bogumil. 2007. African studies: France and the United States. In *The study of Africa: Global and transnational engagements*, ed. Paul Tiyambe Zeleza, 127–46. Dakar, Senegal: Council for the Development of Social Science Research.

Krasner, Stephen D. 1999. *Sovereignty: Organized hypocrisy*. Princeton, NJ: Princeton University Press.

Kristof, Nicholas D. 5 June 2005. A Policy of Rape. *New York Times*.

Levine, Robert. 2000. *Cuban Miami*. New Brunswick, NJ: Rutgers University Press.

Mamdani, Mahmood. 2009. *Saviors and survivors: Darfur, politics, and the War on Terror*. New York, NY: Pantheon Books.

Matory, R. Lorand. 2005. *Black Atlantic religion: Tradition, transnationalism, and matriarchy in the Afro-Brazilian candomble*. Princeton, NJ: Princeton University Press.

Mazrui, Ali. 1986. *The Africans: A triple heritage*. Documentary series. Arlington, VA and Darlington, UK: PBS and BBC.

Medoff, Rafael. 2 May 2005. A statistical link between the Holocaust and Darfur. Letter to the Editor. *Washington Post*. Available from www.washingtonpost.com (accessed 29 October 2009).

Muhammad, Askia. 14 May 2007. Sudanese president answers questions on Darfur. *Final Call* 26 (2). Available from www.finalcall.com/artman/publish/article_3474.shtml (accessed 8 June 2010).

Probst, Peter. 2007. Betwixt and between: African studies in Germany. In *The study of Africa: Global and transnational engagements*, ed. Paul Zeleza, 157–88. Dakar, Senegal: Council for the Development of Social Science Research in Africa.

Rapport, Nigel, and Joanna Overing. 2007. *Social and cultural anthropology: The key concepts*. London, UK: Routledge.

Sartre, Jean-Paul. 1948. *The emotions: Outline of a theory*. New York, NY: Philosophical Library.

Schell, Orville. *Virtual Tibet: Searching for Shangri-La from the Himalayas to Hollywood*. 2000. New York, NY: Metropolitan Books.

Seligman, Charles Gabriel, and Brenda Z. Seligman. 1932. *Pagan tribes of the Nilotic Sudan: Ethnology of Africa*. London, UK: Routledge.

Steidle, Brian. 2007. *The devil came on horseback: Bearing witness to the genocide in Darfur*. New York, NY: PublicAffairs.

Sudan TV. March 2009. *What they are saying about the so-called ICC*. Khartoum, Sudan.

Wheeler, Roxann. 2000. *The complexion of race: Categories of Difference in eighteenth-century British culture*. Philadelphia, PA: University of Pennsylvania Press.

Wirsing, Robert. 2007. The strategic potential of ethnic diasporas: Lessons from Nazi Germany's "Fifth Column." In *Ethnic diasporas and great power strategies in Asia*, ed. Robert Wirsing and Rouben Azizian, 19–67. New Delhi, India: India Research Press.

Yagoub, Adam Sabil. 2005. [قبائل دارفور] (*Darfur's tribes*). Cairo, Egypt: Dar Ghareeb.

Zeleza, Paul. 2007. African diasporas and academics: The struggle for a global epistemic presence. In *The study of Africa: Global and transnational engagements*, ed. Paul Tiyambe Zeleza, 86–112. Dakar, Senegal: Council for the Development of Social Science Research in Africa.

The United States of Africa: A Revisit

By
GEORGE B. N. AYITTEY

Pan-Africanism was developed over the late nineteenth and early twentieth centuries to combat the political subjugation of black people and the vestiges of slavery. Its founding belief is that black peoples share common cultures, problems, and objectives. It was, therefore, imperative for blacks to unite to achieve their objectives. On the African continent, Pan-Africanism became the rallying cry for the struggle for independence from colonial rule. In 1963, the Organization of African Unity (OAU) was established to advance the cause of Pan-Africanism. However, the organization steadily lost credibility and relevance. It was eventually dissolved in 2001. Its replacement, the African Union (AU), is scarcely better. It became hobbled by political intrigues, inflated egos, and personality clashes among its leaders. Nonetheless, the rationale for a united Africa remains strong today. A much better approach lies in configuring a larger African polity in consonance with Africa's own indigenous heritage. As such, a Confederation of African States (CAS) or an African Confederation would be a better configuration.

Keywords: Pan-Africanism; Organization of African Unity (OAU); Kwame Nkrumah; W. E. B. Du Bois; African Union (AU); United States of Africa; confederation

The concept of African unity or unity of the people of Africa has had a long history. It originated from and served as the bedrock of the Pan-African movement in the late nineteenth and early twentieth centuries. Pan-Africanism, as a philosophy, was derived from

George B. N. Ayittey, a native of Ghana, is a distinguished economist at American University and president of the Free Africa Foundation. An internationally renowned authority on Africa, he is the author of Africa Betrayed *(Palgrave Macmillan 1992),* Africa in Chaos: A Comparative History *(Palgrave Macmillan 1999),* Africa Unchained: The Blueprint for Africa's Future *(Palgrave Macmillan 2004), and* Indigenous African Institutions *(Hotei Publishing 2006).* Africa Betrayed *won the H. L. Mencken Award: "Best Book for 1992." He is a frequent contributor to the* Wall Street Journal *and the* Los Angeles Times; *he appears often on CNN and the BBC; and he has testified before many U.S. congressional committees.*

DOI: 10.1177/0002716210378988

the belief that African people share common cultural and racial bonds as well as objectives. Therefore, there was a need to unite to achieve these objectives. The original purpose of Pan-Africanism was racial and cultural. The formal concept was initially developed outside of Africa to fight the vestiges of slavery, colonialism, and discrimination and to secure independence for the colonized people of Africa. In the mid-twentieth century, it became the rallying cry by African nationalist leaders for independence from colonial rule.

Colonial rule was never accepted by Africans. In many parts of Africa, resistance was ferocious. In North Africa, the Arabs of Mauritania revolted in 1905 and killed the French governor, Xavier Coppolani. In 1896, the Ethiopians ousted the Italians at Adowa with furious vindictiveness. Historians have documented the resistance in West Africa of the Sarakolle Kingdom of Mamadou Lamine from 1885 to 1887, the jihad of Ma Ba Tall from 1861 to 1867 in Senegambia, and revolts by the Abe people of the eastern Côte d'Ivoire from 1891 to 1918 and the Asante of Ghana in 1891. Colonial rule was not accepted on the East African coast either. The Maji-Maji revolt in 1890 was a mass movement that encompassed many ethnic groups—the Shambaa, Zaramo, Zigula, Yao, Ngoni, Ngulu, Kwere, Hehe, Kami, Sagara, Makonde, Mbugu, Arab, and Swahili. In addition, a relatively large number of powerful and wealthy merchants vigorously opposed the colonial powers. Among them were Mirambo (from 1871 to 1884) on the great ivory route of Tabora (Tanzania); Msiri in Katanga (from 1860 to 1891); and, until he allied with the Belgians in the Upper Congo, Tippu-Tib in Maniema. In southern Africa, the Sotho and the Zulu (under Shaka) rebelled against colonial domination in the 1880s, and the Shona and the Ndebele did so during the following decade.

Elsewhere in Africa there were sporadic revolts. But African resistance to colonial rule was, in general, weak because of the vast superiority of European weapons. In all, the early colonial years brought political subjugation and humiliation to Africans. Scores of African rulers died on the battlefield; many more were executed or exiled after defeat. Those who signed treaties and remained as protected rulers soon found themselves demoted from king to chief and required to collect taxes or recruit laborers for their French or German overlords. At a later stage, most were dismissed altogether (Manning 1988, 57).

Outside Africa, resistance to slavery mounted, which, together with that against colonialism, culminated in the formation of the Pan-Africanist movement at the dawn of the twentieth century. In 1900, Henry Sylvester Williams, a lawyer from the Caribbean island of Trinidad, organized a Pan-African conference in London to give black people the opportunity to discuss issues facing blacks around the world. The conference was attended by a few, but significant, representatives of Africa and people of African descent from the Caribbean and the United States, as well as whites from Britain.

The original political objective of the meeting was to protest the unequal treatment of blacks in the British colonies as well as in Britain. However, the need to uphold the dignity of African peoples worldwide and to provide them with education and other social services assumed critical importance. In addition, speakers at the conference celebrated aspects of traditional African culture and the great

historical achievements of African peoples. Among the attendees was the influential Pan-African pioneer Edward Wilmot Blyden, a Caribbean-born Liberian
educator, who wrote extensively in the late nineteenth century about the positive
accomplishments of Africans and may have coined the term "Pan-Africanism."

Subsequent Pan-African meetings were organized by distinguished African-
American scholar W. E. B. Du Bois, cofounder of the National Association for
the Advancement of Colored People (NAACP). The aftermath of World War I
(1914–1918) raised serious concerns among blacks in the United States regarding
the well-being of African-American and African soldiers who had served in the
war and the status of former German colonial territories in Africa that had been
captured during the war by Britain, France, and other Allied powers. Du Bois
convened the first Pan-African Congress in Paris in 1919. The congress was held
at the same time as the Paris Peace Conference, at which European powers
negotiated the end of the war.

The agenda of the first Pan-African Congress resembled that of the 1900 conference in its concern for the plight of Africans and people of African descent.
Significant emphasis was placed on the provision of education for Africans and
the need for greater African participation in the affairs of the colonies. This may
be regarded as a precursor to the natives' right to self-determination. Delegates
issued a series of resolutions, one of which was the following:

> The natives of Africa must have the right to participate in the Government as fast as their
> development permits, in conformity with the principle that the Government exists for
> the natives, and not the natives for the Government. They shall at once be allowed to
> participate in local and tribal government, according to ancient usage, and this participa-
> tion shall gradually extend, as education and experience proceed, to the higher offices of
> states; to the end that, in time, Africa is ruled by consent of the Africans. . . . Whenever
> it is proven that African natives are not receiving just treatment at the hands of any state
> or that any State deliberately excludes its civilized citizens or subjects of Negro descent
> from its body politic and culture, it shall be the duty of the League of Nations to bring
> the matter to the notice of the civilized world. (Langley 1979, 740)

The next Pan-African congresses sponsored by Du Bois were held in 1921 (in
London, Paris, and Brussels), 1923 (in London and Lisbon), and 1927 (in New York
City). These congresses were attended by increasing numbers of representatives
from the United States, Europe, Africa, and the Caribbean. Several important factors affected the growing popularity of the congresses. First, many delegates were
sponsored by international labor movements, which were growing in size and
power in the 1920s. A second factor was the growth of the black nationalist movement of Marcus Garvey. The Garvey movement was important in the United
States as a popular expression of the sentiments of African unity and redemption
among working-class blacks. His followers contrasted with the more elite black
groups cultivated by Du Bois. Garvey, a Jamaican, founded the Universal Negro
Improvement Association (UNIA) in 1914 to promote black pride, political and
economic improvements for blacks everywhere, and the repatriation of blacks to
Africa (often called the "Back to Africa" movement).

The Pan-Africanist philosophy, however, subsequently evolved into two forms. A new form, known as Continental Pan-Africanism, emerged to advocate the unity of states and peoples within Africa, either through political union or through international cooperation. This was championed by African nationalist leaders such as Kwame Nkrumah of Ghana during the struggle against colonialism. The other broader form, known as Diaspora Pan-Africanism, retained the original ethos of Pan-Africanism as it related to the solidarity among all black Africans and peoples of black African descent outside the African continent.

On the African continent, new developments were unfolding. In 1945 Pan-Africanists, such as Kwame Nkrumah, George Padmore, and Julius Nyerere, were demanding and pledging equal justice, freedom of the press, freedom of expression, and parliamentary democracy for every part of the continent. The declarations of the Pan-African Congress in Manchester in 1945 were particularly telling: "We are determined to be free. We want education. We want the right to earn a decent living; the right to express our thoughts and emotions, to adopt and create forms of beauty. We will fight in every way we can for freedom, democracy, and social betterment" (Langley 1979, 121).

From 1945 to 1947, Nkrumah served as the general-secretary of the Pan-African Congress and published a monthly paper called the *New African*. The first issue (March 1946) preached African unity and nationalism and attacked imperialism and the unjust laws of the colonies. A prolific writer, Nkrumah authored many books to propagate his ideas and to condemn colonialism. Among his works were "Education and Nationalism in Africa" (1943); *What I Mean by "Positive Action"* (1950); *Ghana: An Autobiography* (1957); and *Africa Must Unite* (1963).

In 1957, Ghana became the first sub-Saharan African state to gain independence, and Nkrumah became its first prime minister. Nkrumah held the Pan-Africanist view that the independence of Ghana would be incomplete without the independence of all of Africa. To work toward this goal, he appointed George Padmore to establish a Pan-African Secretariat within the Ghanaian government. The secretariat pursued the twin goals of total African independence and continental political union in two series of international conferences held between 1958 and 1961. First, the All-African Peoples' Conferences were held to stimulate independence movements in other African colonies. Second, Nkrumah organized the Conferences of Independent African States to establish a diplomatic framework for the political unification of Africa. By inviting representatives from independent North African states to the conferences and by holding the 1961 All-African Peoples' Conference in Cairo, Egypt, Nkrumah's intent was clearly to unite the entire African continent.

In 1960, Nkrumah invited W. E. B. Du Bois to live in Ghana to act as an advisor and to initiate a project that Du Bois had proposed: the *Encyclopedia Africana*, a comprehensive encyclopedia of the culture and history of African peoples. Du Bois died in Ghana in 1963 with this project incomplete. However, the publication of several books during this period made continental Pan-African philosophy more widely known among black people in and outside of Africa. Two notable books were Padmore's *Pan-Africanism or Communism?* (1956) and Nkrumah's *Africa Must Unite* (1963).

In 1960, seventeen African countries gained independence. By the end of 1963, approximately 80 percent of the African continent was independent. Nkrumah's goal of establishing a United States of Africa with a centralized power structure was opposed by the leaders of many of the new African countries, who resisted giving up their nations' newfound autonomy. They were known as the "Casablanca Group." Nonetheless, in May 1963, representatives from thirty-two African nations in both North and sub-Saharan Africa met in Addis Ababa, Ethiopia, and founded the Organization of African Unity (OAU, now the African Union [AU]) as a loose federation of independent African states committed to continent-wide cooperation.

The Organization of African Unity

The OAU started off with a stumble. Right from the beginning, it was hobbled by a number of challenges. First, the independence movement in 1963 was still an "unfinished business." The Portuguese colonies were still not free; they gained their independence in 1975. Rhodesia (Zimbabwe) was still under the colonial yoke until 1980, and apartheid was not dismantled until 1994.[1] Second, there were still political differences among the newly independent African nations regarding the pace of unification. Third, the general lack of resources made it difficult to turn political union into a reality. These factors forced the OAU to shelve political unification, although Nkrumah constantly spoke of it, and to narrow its focus to the liberation of the remaining colonies in Africa.

More significant, the concept of African unity suffered a serious setback—or a near-fatal blow—in 1966 when Nkrumah was overthrown in a military coup in Ghana while on a visit to Hanoi. This event left an enormous leadership vacuum in the Pan-Africanist movement that remained unfilled for decades. Even more distressing was the scarcity of credible leaders to take up the Pan-Africanist mantle. The closest replacements would have been Julius Nyerere of Tanzania and Kenneth Kaunda of Zambia. However, both lacked Nkrumah's charisma and fiery elocution, and both were preoccupied with aiding the struggle against apartheid in South Africa.

Leaderless, the OAU drifted, but continental Pan-Africanism nevertheless remained a dream and a strategy for addressing Africa's economic problems. This was significant because it underscored a more potent rationale for unification—economic integration. Far too many African countries are nonviable economically. Development projects in the 1960s were being duplicated to the point of absurdity. In the race to industrialize Africa, each country was setting up industries with little coordination or reference to each other. For example, it made little economic sense for Côte d'Ivoire, Ghana, Togo, and Benin to each have a cement factory or an airline to serve small local markets. Artificial colonial borders and different currencies were also impeding trade between African nations. Intra-African trade, for decades, has been stuck at 10 percent of Africa's total trade. As a result, in the 1980s, deliberate policies were undertaken to promote regional integration. Regional cooperative organizations were established, such as the Economic Community of West African States (ECOWAS), the East African Economic Community (EAEC), and the Southern African Development Community (SADC, formerly the Southern African Development Coordination Council), which are trade blocs that have played significant roles in regional economic integration. With the increasing pressure of economic competition from international trade blocs in North America, Europe, and Asia, the achievement of economic and political unity on the African continent became an urgent imperative.

However, between 1966 and 2001,[2] the OAU achieved little. During this period, the OAU, plagued with budgetary difficulties and internal wrangling over focus, lost its way. Its focus shifted away from the African people, and its annual summits became a platform for African leaders to grandstand and make grandiloquent speeches. The organization failed to protect the African people from the tyrannical excesses of their leaders. In the process, the OAU rapidly lost both relevance and credibility. The liberation of the former Portuguese colonies in 1975, Zimbabwe in 1980, and South Africa in 1994 did not stem the OAU's slide into ridicule and obscurity. Its performance on conflict resolution, protection of human rights, and promotion of democracy was, to say the least, embarrassing.

It may be recalled that at the Pan-African Congress in Mwanza, Tanzania, in 1958, the delegates bitterly complained that "the democratic nature of the indigenous institutions of the peoples of West Africa has been crushed by obnoxious and oppressive laws and regulations, and replaced by autocratic systems of colonial government which are inimical to the wishes of the people of West Africa." It demanded that "the principle of the Four Freedoms (freedom of speech, press, association and assembly) and the Atlantic Charter be put into practice at once. . . . Democracy must prevail throughout Africa from Senegal to Zanzibar and from Cape to Cairo" (Langley 1979, 780).

The congress stoically resolved to "work for the establishment and perpetuation of true parliamentary democracy in every territory within the African continent." It vowed an "uncompromising safeguarding of liberty of every citizen irrespective of his race, color, religion or national origin." The congress also declared publicly that it was "dedicated to the precepts and practices of democracy." It made it plain that "the safeguards and protection of citizens' rights and human liberties will be buttressed by

- Uncompromising adherence to the rule of law;
- Maintenance of the absolute independence of the judiciary;
- The exercise of the right to vote or stand for any office; and
- The constant observance of the declaration of the Universal Declaration of Human Rights and the United Nations Charter." (Langley 1979, 780)

The delegates also adopted a Freedom Charter that called upon "the Government of East and Central Africa to remove legal restrictions against the freedom of the press and particularly condemn[ed] the unjust prosecutions and convictions which [took] place in some of these Territories against the African Press in particular" (Langley 1979, 780).

After independence, however, the same delegates seldom established those lofty principles and ideals in their own respective countries (Ayittey 1992, 145–76). Instead, they established de facto apartheid regimes, under which political power was monopolized by a head of state and his ethnic group. In 1990, only four out of the fifty-four African countries were democratic: Botswana, The Gambia, Mauritius, and Senegal. By 2008, this number had increased to sixteen, illustrating that the vast majority of African people still lived under repressive, undemocratic systems.

Recall also that the original purpose of Pan-Africanism was to end political subjugation and humiliation of Africans. But the painful irony is that independence did not bring an end to political subjugation and oppression. Independence was in name only. One set of masters (white colonialists) was traded for another set (black neocolonialists), and the oppression and exploitation of the African people continued unabated. Tragically, the OAU never saw this irony or perfidy. It had no active program to promote democracy or freedom in Africa. It defined "freedom" only in racial terms—that is, black Africans were free as long as they were not ruled by white colonialists.

From the 1960s, a brutal campaign of terror was unleashed against the African people by their own leaders. Africans' native freedoms and rights were steadily squashed as brutalities were heaped upon them. They often had no political rights or channels through which to seek redress for their grievances. The police and the army, which were supposed to protect them, instead perpetrated heinous atrocities against them. Uganda offers a classic example, where more than 800,000 people perished at the hands of Idi Amin, Milton Obote, and Tito Okello—all former Ugandan heads of state. When Idi Amin was killing Ugandans at the rate of 150 a day, the OAU did nothing. One Ugandan Anglican bishop, Festo Kivengere, was quite irate:

> The OAU's silence has encouraged and indirectly contributed to the bloodshed in Africa. I mean, the OAU even went so far as to go to Kampala for its summit (in 1975) and make Amin its chairman. And at the very moment the heads of state were meeting in the conference hall, talking about the lack of human rights in southern Africa, three blocks away, in Amin torture chambers, my countrymen's heads were being smashed with sledge hammers and their legs being chopped off with axes. (Lamb 1983, 106)

Amin's reign of terror and slaughter is well known. Less well known but equally infamous was the regime of President Francisco Marcias Nguema of Equatorial Guinea. In 1972, just four years after his country won its independence from Spain, Nguema declared himself president for life. Backed by Cuba, he pursued a policy of systematic extermination of anyone who stood in the way of his attaining absolute power. He expelled Nigerian cocoa farmers to destroy the country's main industry and sank the fishing fleet to prevent anyone from escaping. He declared himself the only god and the "Miracle and Strength" of Equatorial Guinea and demanded that his portrait be placed on every altar. When the Catholic Church refused, Nguema unleashed a campaign of annihilation against his people, who were predominantly (95 percent) Catholic. By the time he was overthrown by a coup in 1979, he had massacred an estimated 50,000 people, or one-seventh of the country's population.

By 1990, the OAU had become irrelevant. Afflicted with an intellectual astigmatism, it could see with eagle-eyed clarity the brutal injustices and atrocities heaped upon blacks by white colonialists and slavers but was hopelessly blind to the equally heinous injustices meted out by African leaders upon their own black people. To the millions of Africans suffering under the repressive yoke of such tyrants as Idi Amin, Francisco Marcias Nguema, Mobutu Sese Seko, Samuel Doe, Sani Abacha, and others, the OAU was irrelevant. It was dismissed as a den of unrepentant despots, noted for its glitzy annual jamborees, where rabid autocrats clicked champagne glasses to celebrate their longevity in office.

Even the late Julius Nyerere, ex-president of Tanzania, became critical of the OAU. In a speech at the University of Edinburgh on October 9, 1997, he excoriated the OAU:

> In a moment of extreme exasperation I once described the OAU as a Trade Union of African Heads of State! We protected one another, whatever we did to our own peoples in our respective countries. To condemn a Mobutu, or Idi Amin or a Bokassa was taboo! It would be regarded as interference in the internal affairs of a fellow African State! (*Chronicle* 2007).

It was this "protection" afforded by its "noninterference clause" that caused the OAU to be conspicuously silent over grotesque violations of human rights in the post-colonial period. But more prominent and eminent Africans started to speak out. On a JOY FM radio interview in Accra, Ghana, in July 2000, Kofi Annan, then UN secretary-general, lamented that sometimes he is "ashamed to be an African" because of the never-ending crises in Africa. At the OAU Summit in Lome, Togo, on July 10, 2000, he blasted African leaders for the mess on the continent. Ghana's state-owned newspaper, *The Daily Graphic*, reported in its editorial:

> At the recent OAU Summit in Lome on July 10, United Nations Secretary General Kofi Annan told African leaders that they are to blame for most of the continent's problems. "Instead of being exploited for the benefit of the people, Africa's mineral resources have been so mismanaged and plundered that they are now the source of our misery." (2000, 5)

Former South African president Nelson Mandela has weighed in, urging Africans to take up arms and overthrow corrupt leaders who accumulated vast personal fortunes while children went hungry. He urged the public to pick up "rifles to defeat the tyrants" (*Washington Post* 2000, A22). Nobel laureate Archbishop Desmond Tutu has added his voice as well. In an interview with the *Saturday Star* in Johannesburg, he said that Zimbabwe's President Mugabe had gone mad, which, he added, was a great sorrow, as Mugabe had been one of the most promising African leaders (2002).

President Thabo Mbeki of South Africa was also sharply critical of African leaders. In 1998, Mbeki called for an end to African leaders' use of state power to gain personal wealth while their citizens continued to suffer in poverty. He went on to say that Africa could not develop and sustain itself if its leaders continued to take for personal gain what should be given to their people. Such a mentality, Mbeki warned, will only keep Africa on the periphery of the global marketplace and stuck in underdevelopment (*The Nigerian* 1998, 28). Mbeki called for an African renaissance:

> We [must] purge ourselves of the parasites and maintain a permanent vigilance against the danger of entrenchment in African society of this rapacious stratum with its social morality according to which everything in society must be organized materially to benefit the few. . . . The call for an African Renaissance is a call to rebellion. We must rebel against the tyrants and the dictators, those who seek to corrupt our societies and steal the wealth that belongs to the people. We must rebel against the ordinary criminals who murder, rape and rob, and conduct war against poverty, ignorance and the backwardness of the children of Africa. (*The Nigerian* 1998, 29)

Continental Pan-Africanism suffered grievously under the auspices of the OAU. Africans could not rally behind tyrannical rulers; there were far too many whom the OAU failed to bring to account. Moreover, it was an incongruous advocate of African unity at a time when many countries were torn by disunity, civil strife, and war. The mandate of the OAU included conflict resolution, and on this, the OAU scored abysmally.

More than forty wars have been fought on the African continent since independence in the 1960s. The economic cost and the human toll have been devastating. Whole states have collapsed, infrastructures have been destroyed, and millions of people have become refugees. By 1994, Africa's refugee count exceeded 10 million, and the death toll from those senseless wars was even greater. Here is a rough breakdown:

- More than 1 million Nigerians perished in the Biafran War of 1967.
- More than 4 million lost their lives in the Sudan's civil wars.
- More than 5 million died in Congo's wars (1996–2003).
- More than 1 million Tutsi were killed in the 1994 Rwandan genocide.

These numbers do not include those killed in the civil wars in Angola, Mozambique, Liberia, Sierra Leone, Côte d'Ivoire, or Burundi. How does one promote continental Pan-Africanism under these circumstances?

The vast majority of these wars have been *intrastate*. Each time a conflict erupted, the instinct of the OAU was to look for a neocolonial or imperialist conspiracy and appeal urgently for international relief aid. The OAU was nowhere to be found when Somalia blew up in 1993. During the 1994 Rwandan genocide in which more than 1 million Tutsi were slaughtered, the OAU was absent. How did the OAU respond to the United Nations request for African peacekeepers in Rwanda? According to the *Washington Post*, "No African nation offered troops. The Organization of African Unity (OAU) chief, Salim Salim, wrote [UN Secretary-General] Boutros-Ghali that the OAU [did] not want to take charge of raising a force, and he passed the burden back to the United Nations" (Preston 1994, A25).

When the war in eastern Zaire erupted in October 1996, the OAU was on vacation. Public outrage forced it to act. It issued a feeble call on the rebels to lay down their arms. The call was ignored, and fighting raged on. Stung and intent on salvaging its reputation, the OAU tried again, convening two conferences in Nairobi. It failed—as did another peace conference that the OAU held in Lome, Togo. It was President Nelson Mandela of South Africa who stepped in to provide some saving grace to the OAU. He convened and presided over a series of meetings between President Sese Seko Mobutu and rebel leader Laurent Kabila in 1997. But Mobutu would not yield or share power, and the country imploded.

The leadership issue, which the OAU had persistently failed to address, was becoming too important to ignore. Eventually, former president Mandela got tired of the antics of the OAU. He skipped the 1998 OAU Summit in Burkina Faso and urged the younger generation of leaders to root out tyranny and put the continent on the information superhighway. "People are being slaughtered to protect tyranny," he said (*News Wires*, June 10, 1998). At the following OAU Summit in Algiers, on July 15, 1999, President Thabo Mbeki of South Africa shocked delegates by stating that African leaders who took power by force would be banned from future OAU summits. Rather than waste time bemoaning the effects of colonialism and globalization, "African leaders should take steps to integrate the continent's economies," he told them. "Mere moral appeals from the have-nots to the haves are not likely to take us very far," he said, encouraging his OAU colleagues "to gain a profound understanding of economics, so that [they could] intervene in an informed manner." Mbeki expressed impatience with those leaders who simply complained that globalization was passing Africa by. He reminded them that little had been done to implement the 1991 Treaty of Abuja that established an African economic community (*Washington Times*, July 15, 1999, A14).

Such straight talk must be applauded as it was urgently needed, not only for the OAU to salvage its credibility but also to push forward the idea of Pan-Africanism. Certainly, this concept cannot be promoted on a continent where the OAU is unable to protect the African people against horrid campaigns of terror, intimidation, and slaughter perpetrated by their own leaders.

The African Union

At the beginning of the new millennium, it became apparent that the OAU had become an irrelevant dinosaur. In March 2001, African leaders gathered in Sirte (Tripoli), Libya, to announce the Declaration of the African Union (Sirte II Declaration) (see Ejime 2001). The declaration was the culmination of seventeen months of work following Sirte I, in 1999, in which the idea for the AU was unveiled. The Sirte II Declaration set out the steps for transforming the OAU into the AU, which was to take place a year later, in 2002.

President Qaddafi hailed the Sirte II Declaration, to be given greater vent at the OAU's 37th summit in July 2001, in Lusaka, Zambia, as the "beginning of a new balance of power" in a unipolar world, where the United States holds sway. OAU

Chairman and Togolese President Gnassingbé Eyadéma, one of the longest-serving African autocrats, described the Sirte II Declaration as "victory and an ambitious step towards the African Union" (Ejime 2001).

In July 2001, Zambia's President Frederick Chiluba welcomed African leaders to Lusaka to consummate the AU, which was to become operational thirty days after thirty-six or two-thirds of OAU members ratified the Constitutive Act. Thirty-two countries ratified the act in Lusaka, while fifty-three countries signed up,[3] excepting Morocco, which had suspended its membership in the OAU because of a western Sahara territorial dispute. Rushing the AU into force without the mandatory ratification would have amounted to an unconstitutional act, hence the compromise on the Sirte II Declaration. Sudanese President Omar al-Bashir told the Pan-African News Agency that it was important to insist on rules to give confidence and legality to the institutions of the AU.

The AU, with a vision of transforming Africa into a closely integrated community, was to be modeled after the European Union (EU). The seventeen components of the AU were to include a Pan-African parliament, a court of justice, a central bank, and a body similar to the United Nations Security Council; the latter was to resolve conflicts on the continent. The second measure taken at Lusaka was the merging of the objectives of promoting Africa's political and economic development into a single project: the Economic Recovery Plan for Africa. Again to induce recalcitrant African leaders to attend, the Libyan strongman paid the overdue OAU membership fees for six African countries, amounting to almost $14 million, and Qaddafi arrived with a delegation of 350.

The new AU did not get off to a good start, already burdened with a $54.53 million debt, representing nonpayment of dues by forty-five of its fifty-three members. The OAU threatened to lock out from the July 2001 Lusaka Summit those member states that had not paid their dues. When Qaddafi settled their arrears, they overwhelmingly approved Qaddafi's concept for the AU. The new AU headquarters was to use the same headquarters as did the OAU in Addis Ababa, Ethiopia.

More threatening to the establishment of the AU were the theatrics, politics of intrigue, machinations of sabotage, and superinflated ego of the mercurial Qaddafi. Libya wanted to host the Pan-African Parliament—one of the seventeen components of the AU—although Libya had no parliament, no military institutions, no political parties, no unions, no nongovernmental organizations (NGOs), and held no elections. Qaddafi described the absence of these key institutions as a permanent revolution. "'In the era of the masses, power is in the hands of people themselves and leaders disappear forever,' he wrote in the Green Book, his published revelations on civil society. Libyans joke that after thirty-one years in power, their leader shows no signs of disappearing any time soon" (MacFarquhar 2001, A1).

A keynote speech by the new AU secretary-general, Amara Essy, to mark the New Year on January 3, 2002, in Addis Ababa, Ethiopia, did not inspire much confidence in the organization. The challenges facing the African continent were both many and complicated, he noted. "The year 2001 has been another difficult year for our continent with its litany of conflicts, tragedies, natural disasters and other hardships linked to poverty and pandemics. . . . The spread of AIDS . . . last year killed more than two million people in Africa. . . . Violation of human rights unfortunately continues to prevail." Then he accused the international community of failing the continent; "their refusal to alleviate Africa's huge debt burden continues to compromise its development," he said (IRIN 2002).[4]

On May 8, 2002, the transformation of the OAU into the AU was postponed—just two months before it was scheduled to happen. Senior officials overseeing the transformation said more time—three to four years—was needed to complete the process of setting up the seventeen key components of the new body, but no time frame within which this process would be completed was given.

Presidential intrigue, fueled by inflated egos, threatened to derail the new AU. "A row over the extraordinary security precautions of Libyan leader [Muammar al-Qaddafi] caused [the] cancellation of a visit to Abuja, Nigeria on February 14, 2001, straining relations between the self-styled architect of African unity and the continent's most populous nation" (*Washington Times*, February 15, 2001, A12).

Over the past two decades, all sorts of grandiose initiatives and megaplans have been announced by African leaders at various summits to launch Africa into the golden age of prosperity. Nothing is subsequently heard of them after the summits. In the late 1980s, there was much excitement about the creation of the African Economic Community. Nothing came out of it. There were other grand initiatives too: the Algerian and South African initiative; the Millennium Partnership for the African Recovery Program (MAP); and the Omega Plan, spearheaded by President Abdoulaye Wade of Senegal. They were integrated into a single plan in 2001 called the Compact for African Recovery by the Economic Commission for Africa (ECA). Subsequently, the Compact metastasized into NEPAD (New Partnership for Africa's Development). All these plans committed African leaders to democratic ideals, establishment of peace, law and order, respect for human rights and basic freedoms, and better management of their economies. They also entreated the international community, especially Western nations, to work in partnership with African leaders to help them to realize their goals.

For example, seeking Western financial support, Presidents Mbeki, Obasanjo, and Wade presented NEPAD—a synthesis of their plans—at the G8 Summit in Genoa, Italy, in 2001. NEPAD sought $64 billion in Western investments in Africa. The official NEPAD document undertook "to respect the global standards of democracy, whose core components include political pluralism, allowing for the existence of several political parties and workers' unions; fair, open, free and democratic elections periodically organised to enable people to choose their leaders freely" (NEPAD 2001, 17). It also included a peer-review mechanism by which African leaders who misruled their countries would be subject to criticism by fellow African leaders according to commonly agreed-upon standards. NEPAD was trumpeted as "Africa's own initiative," "Africa's Plan," "African crafted," and, therefore, "African owned."

However, there were serious problems with NEPAD. First, it turned out NEPAD was modeled after a *foreign* plan: the U.S. Marshall Aid Plan, which rebuilt Europe after World War II. Second, the $64 billion in investments that

NEPAD sought from the West reflected the same old aid dependency syndrome. Third, NEPAD was crafted without consultation with Africa's NGOs and civic groups. At the July 2001 summit in Lusaka, Zambia, the OAU adopted NEPAD as an economic program for Africa to operate as an integral part of the OAU and AU structures and not outside of them. But in December 2001, the NEPAD 15-member Implementation Committee established the NEPAD Secretariat in South Africa—not in Addis Ababa, perhaps out of deference to President Thabo Mbeki, a principal originator of NEPAD—to assist the OAU with transforming itself into the AU. NEPAD had its own structures, procedures, mechanisms, and central organs, separate from the OAU or AU.

In 2001, the West responded positively to NEPAD. Both the United States and Europe committed themselves to expanded development assistance, and Africa was placed at the top of the agenda for the 2002 G8 Summit. But as an editorial in the *Washington Post* pointed out,

> If Africa's new partnership means anything, it is that the continent's leaders must tell Mr. Mugabe to stop terrorizing his country and call fresh elections. But Africa's leaders have equivocated. Mr. Obasanjo and Mr. Mbeki played their part in expelling Zimbabwe from the Commonwealth, much to their credit. But they have not used their partnership as a tool to squeeze him, and Nigeria recently blocked a European attempt to force a vote of censure at the U.N. Human Rights Commission. "There is an urgent need to set up parameters for good governance," Mr. Obasanjo declared at the recent partnership summit. If Mr. Mugabe does not fall outside those parameters, who will take them seriously? (May 6, 2002, A20)

The problem was that the architects of NEPAD did not even take themselves seriously. Instead of working collectively to advance NEPAD as an "African initiative," South Africa spearheaded NEPAD with Nigeria, Algeria, and Senegal, in a group known as "the powerful G4," leaving the other countries chafing with little role to play.

On June 5, 2002, African leaders met in Durban, South Africa, to fine-tune the details of the ambitious recovery plan for Africa. But bitter acrimony engulfed the endeavor, and tension emerged about the powerful G4 core countries steering NEPAD. Irate at being excluded from the core group on allegations of corruption in his government, Kenyan President Daniel arap Moi left in a huff, barely 24 hours after the opening of the summit and without making any formal addresses. His team of government officials subsequently withdrew from panel discussions on NEPAD. Kenya also complained that South Africa was rushing ahead with NEPAD without explaining the program to the rest of Africa. Libyans were also left out. According to an African ambassador, some ministers felt that Libya was still largely isolated internationally; this incensed Qaddafi because "Libya [had been] . . . a major force behind the creation of the AU" (*The Sunday Standard On-Line* 2002).

Hope for the AU was rapidly fading. Professor Adebayo Adedeji, the Nigerian member of the Eminent Persons Panel overseeing the establishment of the AU, hoped that the AU would not be old wine in a new bottle with the "O" removed from the OAU (Ankomah 2002, 22). His hope did not pan out.

By 2010, not only NEPAD but the concept of the United States of Africa was also dead. At the AU Summit in Addis Ababa, Ethiopia, in January 2010, Col. Muammar al-Qaddafi "delivered a rambling rebuke of fellow African heads of state after they chose to replace him as chairman of the African Union and failed to endorse his push for the creation of a United States of Africa" (McLure 2010, A7). South Africa, Ethiopia, and Nigeria were among the countries that opposed Qaddafi's attempts to form a continental government, which many viewed as impractical given the political and economic disparities in Africa.

A More Effective Approach

Without question, the concept of an AU is visionary and imperative for the long-term prosperity of Africa. The multiplicity of artificial boundaries and currencies on the continent impede economic growth, trade, and free movement of people. Qaddafi was right when he argued that individual African states are too weak to negotiate with major powers such as the European Union (EU), the United States, and China. But he bungled the AU idea. What lessons can be learned, and what steps need to be taken to revive it because the idea of a United States of Africa is too important to die?

Lesson 1. The concept of Pan-Africanism or continental unity is too important to be left to the whims of a single leader. Pan-Africanism's fortunes rose and fell with the credibility or eccentricities of the leaders of African states.

The first problem with the AU or the United States of Africa resided with the African leader who actively championed and promoted it—Col. Muammaral Qaddafi of Libya. He lacked democratic credentials. A controversial and mercurial leader, he seized power in Libya in 1969 and has been in power since. An eccentric with an inflated ego, he projected himself as the leader of the Arab world, but the Arabs rejected him. In 1988, he orchestrated the Lockerbie bombing that brought down a Pan Am aircraft, killing 277 passengers and flight crew. He admitted responsibility and paid $2.7 billion in compensation to the victims in 2003.

Qaddafi has ruled Libya erratically with an iron fist and has kept his people in a state of controlled chaos and confusion. Life in Libya is unpredictable. Libya, with a population of five million, earns more than $8 billion annually from oil exports, but no one seems to know what Qaddafi does with the oil money. Roads are cratered with yawning potholes, telephones are unreliable, and there are few private-sector jobs. Most workers are on the public payroll—about 800,000—and have not had a real wage increase in about 20 years. Said Selma Iswid, a housewife addressing a Popular Committee meeting,

> The roads here might as well have been through the war in Chechnya. We are an oil-rich country, we should have better roads. They should put whoever built them on trial. All the facilities are in a very bad shape: services, transportation, health care. We are not satisfied with any of this. (MacFarquhar 2001, A1)

Outside Libya, there were serious questions about Qaddafi's vision and motives for the AU. Ghana's government-owned paper, *The Mirror*, was skeptical about its implementation in an editorial:

> Though the idea is laudable and long overdue, and has received the verbal support of most African leaders, people are very skeptical of its successful implementation considering the fact that the continent is very rich in leaders who are more conscious of their personal gains than leaving foot prints of development during their tenure of office. The idea for [an] economic Union for Africa is a noble one which would have been given serious consideration long ago, but whether [Qaddafi], a man who had just emerged from international isolation, can push hard for its fulfillment is another matter. (2000, 12)

An editorial in another Ghanaian paper, *The Guide*, also questioned the motives of Qaddafi and warned that Qaddafi's "sudden interest in Black Africa especially the United States of Africa is an issue that should not be taken lightly or for granted by the intelligentsia of sub-Saharan Africa" (2000, 6). It would have been far better if the concept of the United States of Africa had been pushed by a commission rather than an individual leader.

Lesson 2. There was considerable confusion over what name the larger configuration of African states should be called: the AU or the United Sates of Africa. Either term was problematic because it sounded "borrowed" or "copied" and thus lacked originality.

Too often in the post-colonial period, African leaders blindly copied foreign systems and transplanted them in Africa. France once had an emperor, so Jean-Bédel Bokassa spent nearly a quarter of the GNP of the Central African Republic (CAR) to crown himself emperor of the CAR in 1979. Rome has a basilica; so too must Africa in Yamassoukrou, Côte d'Ivoire. The United States has a space center, so Nigeria built an $89 million Obasanjo Space Center in 2007. The continent is littered with the putrid carcasses of failed imported systems. Yet the blind copying continues. Europe has the EU; so too must Africa. Never mind that, in 2002, the Europeans had not agreed to the final details of their union. Britain was ambivalent about joining the EU; France wanted EU powers to be more centralized, while Germany favored more decentralization. But a union modeled after the EU, Africa must have. North America has the United States of America, so too must Africa. A far better term would be the Confederation of African States (CAS) or, simply, the African Confederation.

There are three ways in which a large polity can be organized:

1. The *Unitary System*, in which all important decisions are centralized at the capital city—as in the European model.
2. The *Federal System*, in which decision-making is decentralized but the center is still powerful—as in the American model.
3. The *Confederal System*, in which there is much greater decentralization of power and decision-making, and the constituent states have more power than does the center. This is the indigenous African model, and the present-day equivalent is the Swiss canton system.

During colonial rule, the authoritarian colonial state centralized power and all decision-making in the capital. Since the colonial authorities were European, they chose their own unitary state systems, in which decisions were centralized in London, Paris, and Lisbon. After independence, Africa was bequeathed a political model in which Africans of various ethnicities, religions, and cultures were crowded into one state. One would have thought that African leaders would have dismantled the unitary colonial state, and paid respect to their own indigenous heritage, by adopting political configurations that allowed their constituent communities the autonomy that they had enjoyed in pre-colonial times. In fact, America's Founding Fathers drew inspiration from the ancient Iroquois Confederacy. Acoording to Johansen (2009), "immigrants arrived in colonial America seeking freedom and found it in the confederacies of the Iroquois and other Native nations." Instead, virtually all of the African nationalist leaders retained the unitary state system, with the possible exception of Nigeria. But even there, federalism existed only on paper.

As it turned out, the unitary state system was not only unsuitable for Africa's multiethnic and diverse cultures but also became the source of Africa's problems of political instability and turmoil and civil wars. The dangerous concentration of power in the capital has always tempted armed enthusiasts to seize the capital and use that power to enrich themselves, their cronies, and tribesmen and exclude everyone else (the politics of exclusion). This sets the stage for civil war and the eventual implosion of a country. Politically excluded groups have started nearly all of Africa's civil wars since 1960.[5] Furthermore, rebel leaders usually have one place in sight to capture—the capital city—because that is where power lies.

Now, African leaders seek to repeat this monumental political disaster with even *greater concentration of power* by modeling the AU after the EU, where power and decisions are centralized in Brussels. A far better model would be an African Confederation, with extensive devolution of power to reflect Africa's own heritage: the ancient empires of Ghana, Mali, Songhai, and Great Zimbabwe[6] were all confederacies, and they lasted centuries (Ayittey 2006; Diop 1987; Stride and Ifeka 1971). Modern-day Switzerland is a confederation of twenty-three cantons—a much better model for African leaders to copy if they need to satisfy their xenophilic propensities.

There are strict rules for admission into the EU. For example, a prospective member must have a democratic government, and its budget deficit must be within certain limits—less than 6 percent of its gross domestic product. These tough conditions were intended to facilitate the harmonization of fiscal policies in the EU. By contrast, there were no such membership requirements for the AU. Any African state—democratic or not—could join the AU. To be feasible, one would think that a minimum requirement for the AU would be internal unity within each African state. Are the Hutu and Tutsi united in Rwanda and Burundi; are the Hausa and Yoruba in Nigeria; are the Congolese; are the Arabs and black Africans in the Sudan and Mauritania?

Lesson 3. A more pragmatic approach to the AU should start at the regional level: unite those countries in ECOWAS, EAEC, SADC, and so on before moving up to the continental union. In other words, seek modest successes with regional unions and then build upon them for the continental objective.

Continental Pan-Africanism is not dead. It can be revived by avoiding the mistakes that the OAU and the AU have made.

Notes

1. In 1990, then-President F. W. de Klerk announced the end of apartheid, although the first democratic elections, and the official end of apartheid, did not take place until 1994.

2. The OAU was disbanded in 2001.

3. This article includes Spanish Sahara as an African country. The United Nations, however, does not recognize Spanish Sahara as an African country but instead as a non-decolonized territory.

4. See http://www.irinnews.org/IRIN-Africa.aspx.

5. Such politically motivated civil wars include, for example, the Biafran War in Nigeria (1967–1970), the Angolan civil war (1975–2001), the civil wars in Chad (1977–1981), the Mozambican civil war (1975–2001), the civil war in Sierra Leone (1997–1999), and so on.

6. The Ghana, Mali, and Songhai Empires were in current-day West Africa. Great Zimbabwe is an ancient, ruined city, which sits in current-day Zimbabwe.

References

Ankomah, Baffour. 1 June 2002. Funding the union. *New African*.

Ayittey, George B. N. 1992. *Africa betrayed*. New York, NY: St. Martin's.

Ayittey, George B. N. 2006. *Indigenous African institutions*. Dobbs Ferry, NY: Transnational Publishers.

Chronicle (Ghanaian). 7 February 2007. After six years in existence African Union comes under scrutiny.

The Daily Graphic. 12 July 200.

Diop, Cheikh Anta. 1987. *Pre-colonial black Africa*. Chicago, IL: Lawrence Hill Books.

Ejime, Paul. 3 March 2001. Africa makes history with Sirte II Declaration. PanAfrican News Agency. Available from http://allafrica.com (accessed 14 June 2010).

The Guide. 12–18 July 2000.

Integrated Reginal Information Network (IRIN). 2002. Available from www.irinnews.org.

Johansen, Bruce E. 2009. Native American ideas of governance and U.S. constitution. Available from www.america.gov.

Lamb, David. 1983. *The Africans*. New York, NY: Vintage.

Langley, J. Ayo, ed. 1979. *Ideologies of liberation in black Africa, 1856–1970*. London, UK: Rex Collins.

MacFarquhar, Neil. 14 February 2001. Libya under Qaddafi: Disarray is the norm. *New York Times*.

Manning, Patrick. 1988. *Francophone Sub-Saharan Africa l880–1985*. New York, NY: Cambridge University Press.

McLure, Jason. 31 January 2010. After losing a post, Qaddafi rebukes the African Union. *New York Times*.

New Partnership for Africa's Economic Development (NEPAD). October 2001. The African Union.

The Nigerian. October 1998.

Nkrumah, Kwame. 1943. Education and nationalism in Africa. *Educational Outlook* 18 (1): 32–40.

Nkrumah, Kwame. 1950. *What I mean by "positive action."* Accra, Ghana: Ministry of Information and Broadcasting.

Nkrumah, Kwame. 1957. *Ghana: An autobiography*. London, UK: Nelson.

Nkrumah, Kwame. 1963. *Africa must unite*. New York, NY: International Publishers.

Padmore, George. 1956. *Pan-Africanism or communism? The coming struggle for Africa*. London, UK: D. Dobson.

Preston, Julia. 8 May 1994. Rwandans confound U.N. Security Council; humanitarian impulse as mission impossible. *Washington Post*. Available from www.washingtonpost.com.

Stride, G. T., and Caroline Ifeka. 1971. *Peoples and empires of West Africa*. Teaneck, NJ: Holmes & Meier.

Saturday Star. 12 January 2002.

Washington Post. 7 May 2000.

Africa's Development beyond Aid: Getting Out of the Box

This article argues that Africa's development rests not on aid, but on three key pillars: knowledge, entrepreneurship, and governance. Africa needs to think outside of the box when establishing these pillars. However, to make these three levers work, a change in mindset is a prerequisite. Africa has to start dreaming big dreams that empower it to see long-term. Africa must restructure societies so that networks beyond closed ethnic networks are more prominent. The larger social capital that will result will build a foundation for development. Africa also needs to incorporate new actors in its development agenda, including faith-based organizations, the diaspora, and the business class; and it must encourage immigrant entrepreneurs, especially Asians, to come in as chase rabbits. Better governance will come from the transformation of people from subjects to citizens. For success in international trade, Africa needs to learn the lessons of the Savannah, where the effective pack is the king.

Keywords: development; social transformation; inclusive business; trade; governance; aid; diaspora

By
JULIUS GATUNE

Underdevelopment has been the reality for Africa over the past 50 years. The development projects undertaken after independence and underpinned by Western aid have largely failed to deliver. Aid has been disbursed in the trillions,[1] but the statistics have deteriorated in tandem. For instance, the high income per capita growth of 2.2 percent experienced in the

Julius Gatune is a Kenyan with a multidisciplinary background in engineering, computer science, business administration, and policy analysis. He is a research associate at the Frederick S. Pardee Center for the Study of the Longer-Range Future at Boston University. Gatune is also policy advisor to various African governments as a fellow with the African Centre of Economic Transformation (ACET). He holds a PhD in policy analysis from the Pardee RAND Graduate School. Gatune has a particular interest in understanding what Africa needs to transform itself. His other interests include technology diffusion and the role of information and communication technologies in development and inclusive business.

DOI: 10.1177/0002716210378832

1960s plunged to 0 percent by the end of 1970s, averaged –1.76 percent between 1981 and 1985, and stayed in negative territory until 1995 (Fosu 2009). Aid is now seen as the very reason for Africa's underdevelopment (Easterly 2005; Moyo 2009). However, proponents of aid have argued that Africa would have been worse off without it because of the many unfortunate circumstances that Africa inherited upon independence. Such circumstances have put Africa in an under-development trap (Sachs et al. 2004; Collier 2006).

Aid has been pushed to the center of the debate about development in Africa, with extreme positions for and against it. This is unfortunate, as development is not about getting a helping hand to get out of a trap (Sachs et al. 2004) or being denied largesse and thus forced to act responsibly (Moyo 2009). Countries have received massive amounts of aid and done poorly, (e.g., Afghanistan);[2] countries have also received little or no aid and also done poorly (e.g., Somalia). There are also countries that have received aid and done spectacularly well, such as Germany and South Korea. Aid is thus not central to determining the develop-ment path that a country will take. A beggar retires a beggar, but a borrower retires rich: two people who are doing similar things but with different mindsets. Development is about mobilizing resources, acquiring the capacity to utilize the resources, and allocating those resources appropriately. But what mindsets pre-vail determine what path development takes.

For Africa to develop, it has to think in ways that defy conventions. This means that Africa will need to think beyond aid as the central plank of its development plans. It will need transformations in its mindsets. This article seeks to expound on the theme of transformation, drawing from successes in Africa—present and past—to come up with out-of-the-box ideas for how Africa should forge ahead.

Social Transformation

From beggar to borrower

Behavioral economics points to how individuals make economic decisions. Individuals are not necessarily rational; Kahneman (2003) shows that individuals can make different decisions when the same choice is presented in different ways. How concepts and ideas are packaged is a powerful driver of economic behavior (a fact well known to marketers). When offered something for free, as in the case of aid, people tend to undervalue it.

Africa will need to finance its development, and it can find such finances from many sources. The cheapest sources, in terms of interest rates, grace periods, and length of time for repayment, will always be grants and concessionary loans, which are collectively called aid. But the effectiveness of aid hinges on how it is framed. Aid to Africa is currently given as a way of assuaging the guilt of the West and because of outright pity (Collier 2007; Zachary 2009). These are also the same reasons people give to beggars. The very word *aid* reinforces the beggar mental-ity. This mentality[3] is the key challenge for development in Africa. It creates a situation where lenders can give money and also dictate what one should do with that money.

Banks do not give based on charity but on the potential for return. The borrower, being an empowered partner, is not obliged to take all the business advice that the bank gives. The borrower has the space to craft a strategy and implement it in the way he or she sees fit. Africa is viewed more as a beggar than a borrower. Acting like a beggar, Africa has sometimes conceded policy space to its lenders, who have at times forced it to implement harmful policies (Action Aid 2005). It is the transformation from a beggar to a borrower mindset that will allow African policymakers to recover their policy space and begin thinking for themselves. Malawi has demonstrated this kind of change: it has managed to move from a food deficit of 43 percent in 2005 to a 53 percent food surplus in 2007 by thinking for itself (Denning et al. 2009). This surplus was a result of government-subsidized fertilizer given to Malawian farmers against the advice of donors (Dugger 2007).

Dream and dream big

Great leaders have known that grand visions are important and that the images they conjure can drive a country to great heights. The manifest destiny of the United States is a great example, while the idea of the middle kingdom (China as the center of the world) served China well for millennia and is probably at the heart of China's current resurgence on the world stage. Africa needs to dream and to dream in ways that defy current imagination. Most successful people in Africa at one time shared their rooms with livestock, wore shoes for the first time in high school, had their first taste of cereal at university, and so forth. The story of Obama Sr. and his son Barack Obama is the norm in Africa.[4] What Africa needs to do is to move from great individual dreams to great national dreams.

We are seeing a bit of dreaming currently in Africa. The dreams, though, are not grand enough. For instance, Kenya has its Vision 2030 to make it a middle-income country by 2030 on the back of 7 percent annual growth. Rwanda's Vision 2020 program aims to grow its income per capita to $900 by 2020. These are laudable efforts and may be realistic, but they are still constrained in the box of what is thought of as success in the African context. For the past two decades, China has been growing at about 12 percent and from a much higher base than Africa. The growth rates suggested in the cases above do not reflect a desire to get out of the box. We are yet to hear of 15 percent sustained growth rates in Africa.[5]

It is audacious dreams that will remove Africa from its underdevelopment trap. History shows great examples of the kind of audacity in which Africa must indulge. In dreaming of weaving the Abyssinian (Ethiopian) Empire, in the midst of a rising Europe, Emperor Twedoros kidnapped Europeans (detained them as his "guests") and forced them to build a number of cannons for him and teach his people cannon-making skills. Anticipating the Europeans' arrival, Twedoros built a road to move the huge cannons to a formidable, defensive position on the Magdala mountain. A British expeditionary force finally rescued the Europeans in 1868 using a large contingent of soldiers brought from all over the empire and elephants from India, but Twedoros's accomplishments had a powerful impact on the Europeans and other Ethiopians (Mardsen 2007). Twedoros understood that getting critical technology (military technology) from potential adversaries required audacity. Twedoros's audacity earned him respect and inspired generations that followed and may have saved Ethiopia from colonization.[6] This is the "can do" spirit that needs to be imbibed in Africa if it is to develop.

Eritrea: The little train that could

Eritrea is blazing the trail of audacity. Though some of its dreams are misguided,[7] it has demonstrated the power of vision. Eritrea has managed to bring back to life a train system that had been abandoned for more than 25 years, which includes pre–World War II trains. The trains are now a tourist attraction, apart from serving Eritrea. This system was revived using local ingenuity, including recalling engineers in their 70s who had already retired (Orr 1996). The same ingenuity has been shown in the country's maintenance of 1930s Fiat cars, which are now coveted so much by car collectors that Eritrea has banned their export. Eritrea has displayed the right attitude toward technology that all of Africa should. Africa must demystify technology before it can start developing. The sheer hunger for knowledge is a more powerful driver of technology acquisition than any elaborate technology transfer that any donor (or China) may design.

From closed ethnic networks to open society

The wealth of individuals in any society is largely a factor of the social capital embedded in the society that they live in. Social capital is the sum of all networks and the trust within those networks. Nobel laureate Herbert Simon has estimated that social capital is responsible for at least 90 percent of what people earn in wealthy societies like the United States, and more recently, Warren Buffet has been emphatic about the role of social capital in individual wealth (Singer 2006). But these networks and the trust become beneficial only when group membership does not lead to discrimination or exploitation of nonmembers. Trust between members of the group must extend to other groups in society so that beneficial transactions can take place and ideas can be diffused from one group to another. However, social capital is productive only when groups are powerful. Africa suffers from low social capital mainly due to failure of states to deliver their promises of security and opportunity. In the face of weak states, people have turned to ethnic and clan networks for security and opportunity. The result has been fragmented societies.

Closed networks limit interactions and especially entrepreneurship, as value-creating activities tend to be confined to closed communities. The result is that certain ethnic groups dominate certain businesses, such as the Kikuyu in Kenya and Ibo in Nigeria, both of which dominate trading in their respective countries. This domination has the effect of limiting the flow of talent to various sectors, curtailing these sectors' potential. Furthermore, as certain communities grow in wealth, on account of closed information networks, resentment usually follows. This resentment over time can lead to destruction, such as in the case of the expulsion of Indians from Uganda in the early 1970s or Kenya's near implosion following its 2007 elections. Closed ethnic networks create a poisoned political landscape that emphasizes differences between people rather than their commonalities. A country is seen as a commons to be exploited by the various groups, and politics then becomes a vicious competition for state capture to tip the distribution of the commons to the winners. The impact of this uneven distribution is huge on the economic growth rate, contributing up to 35 percent of the observed growth differential in Africa and fostering a culture of corruption (Easterly and Levine 1997; Shleifer and Vishny 1993).

Africa's problems will never be resolved until all ethnic groups see their respective countries not as a common to be extracted for the benefit of their micronations but as theirs to develop. This national identity formation is critical in moving Africa ahead. Wangari Maathai (2009) has proposed teaching children at least one other language in school so that they can better appreciate other communities. South Africa has formally adopted 11 languages as its "official" languages. Other countries have proposed doing away with the tribe identification. Donors in Kenya advised the country to drop the question about tribe in the 2009 national population census (Siringi 2009). However, encouraging people to intermingle is the most effective way to forge a new national identity.

School is a good instrument for achieving a collective national identity. Governments should mandate that all secondary (high) schools enroll students from all ethnic groups on a quota basis. To make this more effective, all schools should be made boarding schools to allow closer contact among students and the development of new identities. Friendships formed at this stage will also create new networks, devoid of tribal identities, networks that will serve them in their youth as well as in their adulthood.

National youth service programs after high school graduation should further consolidate this identity building. National youth services should undertake public projects such as building roads or canals. This will also allow youth to travel to different parts of their countries (and even other countries) and appreciate other cultures. A country's national youth service should serve as a medium for indoctrinating values of public service and nationalism and also provide youth an opportunity to feel valued and continue to develop nonethnic networks. Graduation from a national youth service should be the new rite of passage to adulthood, much as circumcision is in some communities today.

Urbanization is another powerful tool for integrating people. African governments should take an active role in urbanizing their countries. They should look to the example of Singapore, which broke ethnic networks through settling different ethnic groups in new urban centers (Yew 2000). Children growing up in these neighborhoods in Singapore will have nonethnic networks. African governments should also look to examples on their own continent. For example, this approach is being implemented in Rwanda under its *Imidugudu* program and was central in building the strong Tanzanian national identity under the *Ujamaa* program (van Leeuwen 2001). But urbanization in Africa inevitably means growth of megaslums, such as Kibera in Nairobi, Kenya. Slums are a health hazard and pose a serious threat to public safety as they are breeding grounds for crime. But many great cities had such beginnings. Dickens's London was a huge slum, as were many parts of New York City. For example, the Five Points slum of 18th-century New York became a tourist attraction because of its degradation (Chamberlain 2003). In the twenty-first century, Kibera is also a tourist attraction, perhaps for the same reasons (Odede 2010).

Nevertheless, the social capital that will result, because of the greater integration of people in cities, will generate the necessary trust that is needed to grease development. Aid provided to countries with high levels of social capital means that the aid will be better utilized, rather than siphoned off to the group(s) in control. Social capital also makes it easier to mobilize local resources. For example, a national youth service could be deployed to dig an irrigation canal as a public service, rather than having to use aid to do so. Higher trust among people means that lending will be less risky, and thus resources to mobilize and fuel entrepreneurship will be released. Taxes and savings that are generated from increased entrepreneurship are more effective in raising development resources than is aid, as people paying taxes expect and get better services from governments. An integrated, multicultural society is more likely to pursue nationally beneficial projects as opposed to aid-driven projects, which are likely to be in the interest of donors. Integrated societies are also less likely to be skewed to benefit those groups that have the power.

Faith will move mountains

Faith is perhaps the biggest unexplored tool for development in Africa and is far more effective than aid.[8] Beck and Ver (2002) point out that most people in the global South (Africa, Asia, and Latin America) are highly spiritual, and the failure to understand and explore their spirituality reduces the effectiveness of their countries' development. Indeed, the Protestant Reformation has been credited with the rise of Europe. Can religion achieve a similar result in transforming Africa, especially now that Africa is actively shaping the direction of Christianity?[9]

Churches have been and continue to be at the forefront of providing education and health services in Africa. Dowden (2008, 16) argues that churches have supported more real development in Africa than all government and aid agencies combined. Faith groups have also influenced entrepreneurship in Africa. The Mouride Islamic Brotherhood of Senegal, with its central teaching emphasizing self-reliance and entrepreneurship, is a formidable global business force. It has enabled a support network, which links the diaspora and local members in a web that facilitates a global exchange of knowledge, goods, and credit (*The Economist* 2006). It has become one of the strongest communities, economically and politically, in Senegal.

Religious organizations also create broad transethnic and transnational communities, so that when a person moves from city to city or country to country, there is a sort of surrogate family structure already in place (Lester 2002). It is this power that can be used to break ethnic networks that stifle Africa and prevent movement of people and the flow of ideas. By creating new information networks, religious groups also provide means by which the poor or excluded can become part of mainstream business. Equity Bank in Kenya is using such networks to vet the creditworthiness of people who are otherwise outside the conventional credit-rating mechanisms, tapping the huge market of the unbanked in Africa.

The role of faith-based organizations in development could be enhanced further if governments embraced them and channeled public resources through them. A significant percentage of a country's health and education services budget should be channeled to them. This flow will have a tremendous impact on service delivery, as religious organizations have proven to be more efficient than governments in providing services, and the former also tend to better serve the poor.

Brand Africa: Image is key to transformation

Image is an important arsenal in changing mindsets. People's self-images determine what they will aim to achieve (Kebede 2004). Africa's image is a highly confused one. Writers have simultaneously portrayed Africa as innocent and corrupting, savage and pure, and irrational and wise (Zachary 2009). While there are many narratives on Africa (see Zachary 2009), the one that is most harmful to the continent is the victim narrative. This narrative drives the current relationship between Africa and the world and is at the heart of Africa's development policy. In particular, it underpins its aid policy.

Great efforts have been made to make Africa look like the harmless and hapless victim, especially by donor agencies keen to keep their budgets running (Pineau 2005). There is also the general feeling among Africans that some nations want to take advantage of Africa. First, it was the Europeans under colonialism and, later, neocolonialism. Now it is the Chinese who want our commodities. We now hear complaints such as, "The danger is that China will politely rip off Africa, just as the West did" (Mbitiru 2006). And "Chinese investments in Africa are a ploy for the Asian nation to take away Africa's natural resources" (Kamndaya 2010).

Few commentators take note that it is in Australia that China has the biggest mining interests. For instance, in 2007, Chinese companies were funding more than 15 minerals and energy projects in Australia worth US$10 billion, mainly in iron ore, coal, natural gas, and bauxite ore. In 2007, Australia was the biggest supplier to China of iron ore, coal, and alumina (*International Herald Tribune* 2007). Between 2000 and 2006, China's investments in Africa totaled only US$6.6 billion (Wang and Bio-Tchané 2007). The reason we do not get a huge outcry about Chinese investments in Australia is probably because Australia is seen as being able to take care of itself. While there continues to be friction over China's increasing desire to control mining companies in Australia, the language used when discussing this partnership is very different from the language used when discussing China's appetite for African minerals. Words such as "exploitation," "neocolonialism," and "new scramble" are more likely to be used in reference to Africa; whereas words such as "business," "increased tax revenues," and "mutual benefits" are more likely to be used in reference to Chinese dealings in Australia (see *International Herald Tribune* 2007; R. Taylor 2009).

This victim mentality also hampers Africa's policymaking. Opportunities are seen as full of hidden threats that Africans have no way of deciphering without the help of those who are invariably Westerners, advisors, journalists, and NGOs (see Blas and England 2008). This creates a paralysis in Africa's decision-making, increasing the disempowering dependency that has defined Africa.

This victim mentality is currently reflected in the incessant criticism of China's activities in Africa, which is mainly that they are not leading to transfer of know-how and, thus, sustainable development.[10] But why should Africa complain that China is not transferring know-how? Who transferred know-how to China? The image of "victim" attracts sympathy and charity, but it takes away something important for Africa: human agency.

Human agency is people's beliefs about their capabilities to exercise control over events that affect their lives. Unless people believe that they can produce desired effects by their own actions, they have little incentive to act or to persevere in the face of difficulties (see Bandura 2006). The lack of African agency has allowed rock stars and Western leaders to take it upon themselves to eradicate Africa's poverty without African involvement (Mugabane 2007).[11] The message that is lacking is that Africans have the will, however constrained by the past, to change their societies for the better (Lonsdale 2005).

History is the most powerful and unused tool in Africa's arsenal. Africans are currently taught a history that is overtly and covertly focused on European achievements and their domination of Africa, peppered with some triumphs from African independence struggles, followed by African failures during neocolonialism, cold war struggles, and debt burdens. It is a story that is at the very least disempowering. Few Africans know of Africa's contribution to the current global civilization, from Egypt's transmission of civilization to the Greeks (Davidson 1994; Bernal 1987); to saving the Judeo-Christian religion, the foundation of the Western civilization (Aubin 2002); to the more recent trans-Sahara gold trade, which fueled the rise of Europe via Genoan and Venetian merchants (Davidson 1994).

People with great histories set the bar for achievement very high. Indeed, the West has gone to great efforts to hide its huge export of Anglo-Saxon slaves to the more advanced Middle East at the height of Islamic civilization (Harris 2004). Few Europeans know of the more than 700 years of Arab colonization of parts of Western Europe and the Arabs' role in passing on knowledge that was the basis for the European Renaissance.

Building Africa's Knowledge Base

Human capacity is needed to formulate and implement development plans. Africa has suffered from lack of capacity, relying heavily on technical assistance that is part of aid packages. Africa needs to rethink how it acquires human capacity and accelerate that process. Increasing skills that are needed to develop Africa will come from expanding access to knowledge and stemming brain drain.

Quantity first versus quality later

Africa has limited resources for the education of its people. The result is a tension between increasing access and increasing quality, especially in higher education. For instance, Kenya has seen explosive growth in university education. This growth has been fueled by intensification in use of university facilities, such as running parallel degree programs in the evenings and geographical expansion, mainly by franchising degree programs to non-degree-granting training institutes.[12] This growth, however, has also been said to have lowered the quality of education in Kenya. While this is probably the case, low quality may not be so costly. A 2005 McKinsey study reports that human resource managers in multinational companies consider only 10 percent of Chinese engineers and 25 percent of Indian engineers as even "employable," compared with 81 percent of American engineers (Pei 2009). Yet China and India are seen as models of growth.

Apart from imparting skills, the other key advantage of higher education is that it confers higher aspirations and expectations (and also frustrations).[13] Ghana's independence was hastened by agitation from a huge number of educated Ghanaians who could not get a job; they were the foot soldiers of Kwame Nkrumah (Rodney 1973). As more people get university degrees—even low-quality ones—they expect better lifestyles and become uncomfortable with the status quo. Education, even if it is of low quality, goes a long way in transforming mindsets. Africa needs a huge number of people refusing to accept poverty as a way of life.

Follow the drain and recover the brain

Africa suffers from a huge brain drain to the West, especially in the areas of science and technology. It is estimated that Africa loses an average of 70,000 skilled personnel a year to developed countries in this brain drain (Commission for Africa 2005). The West lures them with better professional development opportunities and better lifestyles. African countries can recover the lost brains through innovative thinking. Countries can create research institutes in global centers of research and send their scientists to work there. This is the approach that Cuba has taken in the past. Crippled by an economic crisis after the fall of the Soviet Union, Cuba sent its scientists to Sweden, Germany, and Spain so that they could continue working (Yee 2003). If African scientists can work on African problems in African-funded labs established in more advanced countries, this will turn brain drain on its head.

Knowledge can come from unusual places

Africa needs to take lessons from Asia's success stories. Korea received skills training in management from the Philippines and Pakistan. Malaysia trained its administration staff in Kenya, and more recently, Vietnam obtained its expertise in coffee growing from Kenya. These lessons are being learned. Kenya tax authorities have acquired a state-of-the-art national revenue collection computer system from Senegal. Nigeria has been able to develop a drug to cure sickle cell anemia by studying traditional herbal remedies (*The Economist* 2007). Knowledge can, thus, come from unusual places.

Building Entrepreneurship

There is gold at the bottom of the pyramid

Entrepreneurship is the key engine of growth. While subsistence has generally defined the landscape of Africa, this is not a reflection of lack of entrepreneurial capacity. Bates (1984) notes that the African zeal for entrepreneurship so scared the colonial powers that they went to great efforts to kill it. Generally, lack of access to credit and unsupportive legal and business environments have limited the growth of entrepreneurship in Africa. However, the key obstacle to entrepreneurship is poverty. The majority of Africans subsist on less than $2 per day. However, to an entrepreneur, $2 means 700-million-plus Africans spending more than $1.4 billion per day. This provides a huge opportunity, since the poor tend to pay more for goods and services than the rest of a society.[14] The poor provide a huge market (a fortune) for those with the right models (see Prahalad 2006).

But this is a market that is extremely difficult to crack for conventional businesses, mainly due to lack of credit and access. Innovations are, however, making it possible to profitably do business with the poor. Microcredit and micropayments are making it easy to include the poor in financial systems. Social marketing, where NGOs, community organizations, and governmental agencies work together with business organizations to educate and inform communities about products that can improve their lives, is providing easier access to poor markets.[15] The result is inclusive business where the poor get to be part of business chains as suppliers and as consumers. The net impact is growth of entrepreneurship, resulting in more empowered people and higher taxes.

African governments can do more to promote inclusiveness. Governments are usually the biggest buyers of goods and services in most African countries. They have huge leverage in developing the model. Governments can, for example, mandate that a certain portion of business be reserved for the disadvantaged, as is the case with the 2003 Broad-Based Black Economic Empowerment Act in South Africa (see Republic of South Africa 2004).[16] Governments can create incentives such as tax breaks to entice businesses to adopt inclusive business models.

Wake up the dead capital

Africa has vast amounts of capital that De Soto (2001) refers to as "dead capital." This is capital that cannot be mobilized because property rights are nonexistent.

For most people in Africa, land tenure is nonexistent. The figures for customary land ownership in Southern Africa are as follows: Mozambique, 93 percent; Zambia, 89 percent; Angola, 88 percent; Tanzania, 84 percent (United Nations Environment Program 2006, 107). These numbers indicate that land is not an asset that can be mobilized for entrepreneurship; therefore, people are locked in subsistence. This also makes real estate, a huge sector in many developed economies, nonexistent in Africa. This is the low-hanging fruit that can be reaped at the stroke of a pen through legal reforms.

Imigration: Let the chase rabbits come in

For many in Africa, emmigration is about leaving Africa for greener pastures. But Africa for some is the greener pasture. Indians and Chinese in particular see Africa as a place of opportunity. The use of bribery (Kenya) and subterfuge (Rwanda)[17] and other tricks used to stay in African countries is a testimony to this.

Immigrants are important for the countries to which they immigrate because they bring an entrepreneurial spirit, managerial and technical skills, and new networks. The coming of Chinese, Indians, and other Asians to Africa should be welcomed. Immigrants may compete with the locals for jobs and raise tensions, but it is these tensions that finally awaken locals and force them to learn and to imitate. Immigrants may have better international networks, but locals have better local networks. Local peoples, with time, will demystify the immigrants and learn how to compete. The immigrants are really the equivalent of a chase rabbit that encourages athletes to break world records. The relative sophistication of countries such as Mauritius, South Africa, and even Kenya is due to the presence of significant groups of immigrants.

In the diaspora we have a powerful unexploited web

"When the spider webs unite, they can tie up a lion"

—Ethiopian proverb

The African diaspora, the recent and not so recent, is the vast resource that Africa must exploit. African immigrants are already sending more resources back to Africa than total aid flows; their impact is such that for some countries, such as Lesotho, remittances stand at 28 percent of GDP (Gupta, Pattillo, and Wagh 2007). It is less well studied that the diaspora is playing a powerful role in demystifying the West, transferring key skills back home, and creating important networks that link Africa to the larger world.

Africa can also benefit from the African-American communities that have historical ties to it. In African-American communities, we have personalities that have run big cities and big corporations, we have renowned scientists and engineers, yet in Africa we have a dearth of skills. Developing mechanisms to tap into these communities' knowledge bases could be a powerful driver of development in

Africa. Indeed, the Chinese community abroad, particularly the Guanxi network, has contributed greatly to the rise of China, mainly through knowledge and skills transfers and patriotic investments (Fenby 2008).

Africa needs to do more to incorporate the African diaspora in its communities. As a start, it should provide citizenship or special status to all Africans living away from Africa, much as India has provided special status to its diaspora irrespective of how many decades they have been away. Africa must assiduously court African-American investors, tourists, students, and so forth. Ghana has embarked on this journey (Quist-Arcton 2006). Kenya has a special school for at-risk students from a predominantly African-American Baltimore City public school system (Daly 2005).

Globalization means new and many opportunities for the hunters

Africa supplies a huge proportion of the commodities needed to power the world economies, yet it accounts for less than 3 percent of the global trade. This small percentage partly stems from the way that Africa was integrated into world trade by the colonial powers. The key reason, however, is that Africa has failed to diversify and compete. But this very small share of global trade also means that Africa has huge room to grow. Africa can do this by learning a few lessons from its backyard: the Savannah.

In the Savannah the pack is the king

Animals, whether the mighty lion or the lowly hyena, often hunt in packs. They are also highly focused once they make the choice to hunt. In the global marketplace, Africa has to implement these lessons. Trade is all about forming effective packs and negotiating the terms of trade as a pack. It is also about focusing on developing key competencies, traditional or new, as need be. Africa does not have effective packs, with many countries belonging to at least four trade bodies (Economic Commission for Africa 2004). Being part of too many packs is a sure way to lose focus. This situation is further compounded by African countries' lack of resources to negotiate and to staff their many trade missions (Schiff and Winters 2003).

The hare cannot represent the tortoise

Africa must do more to develop its own negotiating capacity. In international negotiations, especially in the World Trade Organization (WTO), it has been noted that African negotiations are supported by international NGOs (Jensen and Gibbon 2007). WTO negotiations are about fighting for concessions from the West, which has traditionally skewed trade to its own advantage. The West funds most of the NGOs operating in Africa. Therefore, any negotiating advice that the NGOs offer cannot be fully objective.

In the Savannah there are many water holes

Though Africa's share of global trade is small, the trade patterns for Africa seem to be improving. Asia, especially China, is becoming a more important trade partner. This partnership is good, but only if Africa relates strategically to Asia as well as to the rest of the world. Africa should find ways to integrate strongly with all the regions of the world. Fixating on any one country or bloc, as seems to be happening with China, is wrong. Africa should think about what it can get from where and do what is needed to make it work. For instance, Brazil, an agriculturally successful tropical country, can provide agricultural or agro-processing technology to Africa, while Cuba has great lessons to share in improving the health sector.

Putting Governance Basics in Place

Africa's poor performance can largely be attributed to governance. Governance is central to a country's development. It allows the optimal allocation of resources and also creates the environment needed for development activities to take place. The foundation of governance is having a proper principal-agent relationship where the principal (the citizen) has the ability to monitor the agent (the ruler) and ensure that the agent delivers. The key prerequisite for this is a justice system that allows agents to act cooperatively and in a stable environment.

From subjects to citizens

Good governance in Africa will come from the transformation of people from subjects to citizens. The master-subject relationship is a colonial legacy that still exists (Mamdani 1996). The very word for "government" in Kiswahili, *Serikali*, literally means "great secret." This is what the government is in many African countries, a great secret. This mindset allows a lack of accountability and a culture of impunity to thrive. The transition from subject to citizen will be greatly aided by transitions from highly centralized governments to more empowered local governments. Local governments allow citizens to more effectively participate in decision-making because local issues can be more easily grasped. The Kenyan experiment of distributing a proportion of the national budget to constituencies under the Constituency Development Fund (CDF) program is a step in this direction. Though systems for making it work properly are yet to be put in place, it has greatly improved people's level of participation in governance— transforming them into active citizens—and forced greater accountability of leaders at local levels (see Maathai 2009).

Back to the future

Africa has constitutions that are rooted in either Anglo-Saxon or French models, which create poor foundations and continue the legacies of colonialism. They are not rooted on any ancestral standards and thus do not draw from the many institutions of leadership Africa had before colonialism; in that sense they lack legitimacy (Mazrui 2002). Justice systems that have emerged have strange formalities and lengthy procedures far removed from the African reality and experience.[18] These systems require substantial resources in terms of court officers, courthouses, and so forth—resources that many countries find it hard to afford. The result is highly inefficient justice systems. For instance, in 1991, of the 60,000 inmates in Nigeria's state prisons, at least half had never seen a judge (Bach 2006, 76); while at the time of this writing, the number of pending court cases in Kenya was greater than 800,000 (*Daily Nation* 2010).

Inefficient justice systems encourage people to seek justice through private institutions.[19] However, private protection systems are limited in that they can operate only in small networks, and as they grow they can easily morph into mafias (Leeson and Boettke 2009). This has already happened with the *Mungiki* mafia in Kenya. Frustration with inefficient justice systems has led some Nigerian states to adopt the Islamic Sharia legal system (Bach 2006).

Africa needs to rethink its legal system. Rwanda, faced with a huge number of cases as a result of the genocide, has pointed the way forward by reviving a traditional justice system called *Gacaca*. The *Gacaca* has tried more than 1.1 million genocide cases in *Gacaca* courts, while similar trials in Arusha under international law have tried fewer than 44 suspects since 1994, using close to 12 percent of Rwanda's annual budget (Hirondelle News Agency 2006; BBC News 2008).

The *Gacaca* system has been viewed with skepticism, especially in the West, due to its use of laypeople as judges. Rwanda has shown great courage in going back to its traditional systems of justice, knowing that justice existed before the advent of colonialism and Western legal code. It is this kind of courage that Africa needs.

Conclusion

Aid has been the key lever for getting Africa out of its development trap. The application of aid in Africa has, however, not eradicated its poverty. As Africa faces the next 50 years, it needs to reexamine existing orthodoxies and develop new mindsets that will underpin its development path. This is not to say that Africa should take a dogmatic position against aid or the West but that it should have the view that new ideas can come from anywhere, and traditional approaches will not be enough. Africa must get out of the box that has informed its development policies. The key to development is developing mindsets that bring back agency to Africans.

Notes

1. Richard Dowden of the Royal African Society puts the figure at around $1 trillion in aid over the past 50 years, roughly $5,000 for every African living today, if distributed evenly at 2005 prices (I. Taylor 2005). But others have put it at around $500 billion (Easterly 2005).

2. In the past eight years, upwards of $32 billion has been given (*The Economist* 2009, 21).

3. The beggar mentality has become so ingrained in the African mindset that when Kenya was removed from the Heavily Indebted Poor Countries list, rather than celebrate its graduation from kindergarten to elementary school in the Western development paradigm, it complained bitterly because this meant that it could not qualify for debt relief and new grants.

4. Africa is full of stories of dreams come true. Most of the people in high positions come from very humble backgrounds. A person familiar with the chief justice of Kenya told me that the chief justice dressed for one year in a girl's school uniform, because the tailor had made a mistake and mistook him for a girl when his mother went to fit him for his first uniform. Given the level of poverty at this period in Kenyan history, he had to endure the school year dressed as a girl because his mother could not afford to buy another uniform. Unfortunately for Africa, many Africans tend to view their humble past as an embarrass-ment, rather than seeing their rise as an achievement, and such inspiring stories are never told. Obama Sr. went from being a goat herder to Harvard. This is not spectacular for those who live in Africa. Any African president, CEO, or judge, for example, is more likely to come from an even more difficult background than that of Obama Sr.

5. Oil-rich Angola and Equatorial Guinea have attained growth rates of more than 20 percent per annum in the recent years that saw huge surges in oil prices.

6. Twedoros, however, was defeated and committed suicide from the humiliation of defeat. But his memories and accomplishments continued to inspire Ethiopians. Menelik, a protégé of Twedoros, embraced the technology and gadgetry of Europeans and was able to humiliate the Italians at the battle of Adoa in 1896, putting an end to Italy's ambition of colonizing Ethiopia (see Mardsen 2007).

7. Eritrea shuns aid, foments the rebellion in Somalia, and has a tense relationship with Ethiopia.

8. Note that aid is also channeled through religious organizations. So the argument here is not for one against the other but that religion provides a good foundation for building development programs. If aid is channeled through faith-based organizations, it is more likely to be effective. Even without delivering aid, these organizations are good at mobilizing people and developing social capital.

9. The second most powerful person in the Anglican Church, the archbishop of York, is a Ugandan, while Nigeria has a papal contender in Cardinal Arinze (Jenkins 2002).

10. In some instances, especially where grants are involved, China imports all materials and labor. It delivers the final product without the involvement of local workers at any level.

11. Mugabane (2007) argues that this harkens back to the colonial period, when it was believed that Africa was for the white man to shape.

12. Universities have now adopted a fast-food-like franchising model in Kenya.

13. Kahl (1998) argues that the high expectations among educated urban youth in Kenya caused frus-tration and antistate grievance when unemployment hit this group at the end of the 1980s.

14. In Kibera slums, for instance, slum dwellers pay 10 times more for water than do their wealthy neighbors.

15. An illustration of this would be if a soap manufacturer, NGOs, and government agencies concerned with health worked together to inform the poor about the importance of washing hands. In this case, if the social marketing campaign were successful, the poor would benefit from better health, and the business would benefit from higher sales of soap. The sale of the soap could be initially done through micro-businesses. The NGOs and government agencies benefit from tapping the business organization's experience in communication, logistics, and management; while the business mutually benefits from using the NGOs' and governments' infrastructures and specialized local knowledge to access these difficult markets. See Prahalad (2006) for examples of inclusive business. This cooperation also increases understanding between these key agents of development, leading to better coordination and higher impact of development efforts.

16. The overarching stipulation of this 2003 act is to "promot[e] economic transformation in order to enable meaningful participation of black people in the economy." For its other objectives, see Republic of South Africa (2004).

17. Rwanda has a zero-tolerance policy on corruption, but it has very lax rules on investments. It costs about $5 to register as an investor, and using this status, one can get a residence permit. Chinese and others are exploiting this system to masquerade as investors, while their real intentions are to become traders. The minister in charge of immigration in Kenya has also been accused of fraudulently giving stay permits to Indians.

18. Many judges in Africa still wear horsehair wigs, and mayors have worn 16th-century English hats to display authority. We are likely to laugh at a judge dressed in headwear and a robe made from a Colobus monkey skin, the traditional mark of authority in the Kikuyu tribe in Kenya (see Mwai and Muriuki 2003), because that is seen as primitive, but we find it acceptable to don centuries-old English attire.

19. Private institutions embedded in societies are governed by trust, expectations, and norms. They rely on reputation systems and cultural sanctions, such as ostracism.

References

ActionAid. 2005. *Real Aid: An Agenda for Making Aid Work*. Johannesburg, South Africa: ActionAid. Available from www.reliefweb.int/rw/lib.nsf/db900sid/EVIU-6CXB8L/$file/real_aid_may_05.pdf?openelement (accessed 18 June 2010).

Aubin, Henry Trocme. 2002. *The rescue of jerusalem: The alliance of Hebrews and Africans in 701 BC*. New York, NY: Soho Press.

Bach, Daniel C. 2006. Inching towards a country without a state: Prebendalism, violence and state betrayal in Nigeria. In *Big African states: Angola, DRC, Ethiopia, Nigeria, South Africa, Sudan*, ed. Christopher Clapham, Jeffrey Herbst, and Greg Mills, 63–96. Johannesburg, South Africa: Wits University Press.

Bandura, Albert. 2006. Toward a psychology of human agency. *Perspectives on Psychological Science* 1 (2): 164–80.

Bates, Robert H. 1984. Some conventional orthodoxies in the study of agrarian change. *World Politics* 36 (2): 234–54.

BBC News. 18 December 2008. Q&A: Rwanda's long search for justice.

Beck, Kurin, and Alan Ver. 2002. Spirituality: A development taboo. In *Development and culture*, ed. Deborah Eade. Oxford, UK: Oxfam and World Faiths Dialogue on Development.

Bernal, Martin. 1987. *Black Athena: The Afroasiatic roots of classical civilization*. New Brunswick, NJ: Rutgers University Press.

Blas, Javier, and Andrew England. 20 August 2008. Arable land, the new Gold Rush: African and poor countries cautioned. *Financial Times*.

Chamberlain, Ted. 24 March 2003. Gangs of New York: Fact vs. fiction. *National Geographic News*.

Collier, Paul. 2006. African growth: Why a "Big Push"? *Journal of African Economies* 15 (Suppl. 2): 188–211.

Collier, Paul. 2007. *The bottom billion*. New York, NY: Oxford University Press.

Commission for Africa. 2005. *Our common interest: A report of the commission for Africa*. London, UK: Department for International Development.

Daily Nation. 28 April 2010. Kenya: Team's proposals to speed up wheels of justice. Available from http://allafrica.com/stories/201004281019.html (accessed 22 June 2010).

Daly, Emma. 31 August 2005. From Baltimore's streets to Kenya and back. *New York Times*.

Davidson, Basil. 1994. *The search for Africa: History, culture, politics*. New York, NY: Crown.

Denning, Glenn, Patrick Kabambe, Pedro Sanchez, Alia Malik, Rafael Flor, Rebbie Harawa, Phelire Nkhoma, Colleen Zamba, Clement Banda, Chrispin Magombo, et al. 2009. Input subsidies to improve smallholder maize productivity in Malawi: Toward an African green revolution. *PLoS Biology* 7 (1): 0002–0010.

De Soto, Hernando. 2001. *The mystery of capital: Why capitalism triumphs in the West and fails everywhere else*. London, UK: Black Swan.

Dowden, Richard. 2008. *Africa: Altered states, ordinary miracles*. London, UK: Portobello Books.

Dugger, Celia W. 2 December 2007. Ending famine, simply by ignoring the experts. *New York Times*.

Easterly, William. 2005. Reliving the '50s: Poverty traps, the big push, and takeoffs in economic development. Center for Global Development Working Paper 65, Washington, DC.

Easterly, William, and Ross Levine. 1997. Africa's growth tragedy: Policies and ethnic divisions. *Quarterly Journal of Economics* 112 (4): 1203–50.

Economic Commission for Africa. 2004. *Assessing regional integration in Africa*. Addis Ababa, Ethiopia: Economic Commission for Africa.

The Economist. 19 December 2006. Europe's Senegal connection: Faith in the market.

The Economist. 3 February 2007. Local heroes.

The Economist. 20 August 2009. Afghans at the polls.

Fenby, Jonathan. 2008. *History of modern China: The fall and the rise of a great power, 1850–2008*. London, UK: Allen Lane.

Fosu, A. Kwasi. 2009. Understanding the African growth record: The importance of policy syndromes and governance. World Institute for Development Research Discussion Paper no. 2009/02, Helsinki, Finland.

Gupta, Sanjeev, Catherine Pattillo, and Smita Wagh. 2007. Impact of remittances on poverty and financial development in Sub-Saharan Africa. IMF Working paper WP/07/38, Washington DC.

Harris, Nigel. 2004. Book review: Trade in early India: Themes in Indian history, edited by Ranabir Chakravarti and Origins of the European Economy: Communications and Commerce AD 300–900, Michael McCormick. *Historical Materialism* 12 (4): 455–62.

Hirondelle News Agency. 12 May 2006. Rwanda: Cost of the ICTR to reach $1 billion by the end of 2007. Available from http://allafrica.com/stories/200605120745.html (accessed 22 June 2010).

International Herald Tribune. 13 February 2007. Chinese steel companies seek stakes in Australian iron ore projects.

Jenkins, Philip. October 2002. The next Christianity. *Atlantic Monthly*.

Jensen, Michael Friis, and Peter Gibbon. 2007. Africa and the WTO Doha Round: An overview. *Development Policy Review* 25 (1): 5–24.

Kahl, Colin H. 1998. Population growth, environmental degradation, and state-sponsored violence: The case of Kenya, 1991–93. *International Security* 23 (2): 80–119.

Kahneman, Daniel. 2003. A perspective on intuitive judgment: Mapping bounded rationality. *American Psychologist* 58 (9): 697–720.

Kamndaya, Samuel. 30 January 2010. Tanzania: Expert—China hungry for African resources. *The Citizen*. Available from http://allafrica.com/stories/201001300009.html (accessed 20 June 2010).

Kebede, Messay. 2004. African development and the primacy of mental decolonization. *Africa Development* 29 (1): 107–30.

Leeson, Peter T., and Peter J. Boettke. 2009. Two-tiered entrepreneurship and economic development. *International Review of Law and Economics* 29 (3): 252–59.

Lester, Toby. February 2002. Oh, gods! *The Atlantic*.

Lonsdale, John. 2005. How to study Africa: From victimhood to agency. *Open Democracy*. Available from www.opendemocracy.net (accessed 18 June 2010).

Maathai, Wangari. 2009. *The challenge for Africa*. New York, NY: Pantheon.

Mamdani, Mahmood. 1996. *Citizen and Subject: Contemporary Africa and the legacy of late colonialism*. Princeton, NJ: Princeton University Press.

Marsden, Philip. 2007. *The barefoot emperor: An Ethiopian tragedy*. New York, NY: HarperCollins.

Mazrui, Ali A. 2002. Who killed democracy in Africa? Clues of the past, concerns of the future. *Development Policy Management Network Bulletin* 9 (1): 15–23.

Mbitiru, Chege. 12 June 2006. Questions over China's close ties with Africa. *Daily Nation*.

Mugabane, Zine. 2007. Brand the beloved country: Africa in celebrity culture. *CODESRIA Bulletin* 1–2:4–8. Dakar, Senegal: CODESRIA.

Mwai, Muthui, and Muriithi Muriuki. 16 June 2003 President Kibaki installed in symbolic ceremony. *Daily Nation*. Available from http://allafrica.com/stories/200306160497.html (accessed 28 June 2010).

Odede, Kennedy. 9 August 2020. Slumdog tourism. *New York Times*.

Orr, David. 7 August 1996. Old timers put eritrea's trains back on the rails. *The Independent*.

Pei, Minxin. July/August 2009. Think again: Asia's rise. *Foreign Policy*.

Pineau, Carol. 17 April 2005. A changing continent: The Africa you never see. *Washington Post*, B02.

Prahalad, C. K. 2006. *The fortune at the bottom of the pyramid: Eradicating poverty through profits*. Upper Saddle River, NJ: Wharton School Publishing.

Quist-Arcton, Ofeibea. 6 March 2006. Ghana seeks African-American dollars, skills. *National Public Radio (NPR)*.

Republic of South Africa. 9 January 2004. Broad-Based Black Economic Empowerment Act, no. 53, 2003. *Government Gazette*. Cape Town: Republic of South Africa.

Rodney, Walter. 1973. *How Europe underdeveloped Africa*. London, UK: Bogle-L'Ouverture.

Sachs, Jeffrey D., John W. McArthur, Guido Schmidt-Traub, Margaret Kruk, Chandrika Bahadur, Michael Faye, and Gordon McCord. 2004. Ending Africa's poverty trap. Brookings Papers on Economic Activity, 1, Brookings Institution, Washington, DC.

Schiff, Maurice, and L. Alan Winters. 2003. *Regional integration and development*. New York, NY: World Bank and Oxford University Press.

Shleifer, Andrei, and Robert Vishny. 1993. Corruption and economic growth. *Quarterly Journal of Economics* 108 (3): 599–612.

Singer, Peter. 17 December 2006. What should a billionaire give—And what should you? *New York Times*.

Siringi, Samuel. 27 June 2009. Kenya: Controversy over inclusion of tribal identity in census. *Daily Nation*.

Taylor, Ian. 2005. Advice is judged by results, not by intentions: Why Gordon Brown is wrong about Africa. *International Affairs* 81 (2): 299–310.

Taylor, Robert. 18 July 2009. Australia mustn't "Lose Face" in Rio row with China. *Reuters*. Available from www.reuters.com.

United National Environment Program, Division of Early Warning and Assessment. 2006. *Africa environment outlook 2*. Nairobi, Kenya: United Nations Environment Program, Division of Early Warning and Assessment.

van Leeuwen, Mathijs. 2001. Rwanda's imidugudu programme and earlier experiences with villagisation and resettlement in East Africa. *Journal of Modern African Studies* 39 (4): 623–44.

Wang, Jian-Ye, and Abdoulaye Bio-Tchané. 2007. Burgeoning Ties with China. *Finance & Development* 45 (1): 44–47.

World Bank. 2010. *Financing higher education in Africa*. Washington, DC: International Bank for Reconstruction and Development and World Bank.

Yee, Chen. 17 April 2003. Cutting-edge biotech in old-world Cuba. *The Christian Science monitor*.

Yew, Lee Kuan. 2000. *From third world to first: The Singapore story 1965–2000*. New York, NY: HarperCollins.

Zachary, G. Pascal. 2009. *Stories we tell about Africa (and those we don't)*. Available from www.gpascalzachary.com/bio.htm (accessed 25 August 2009).

Afrocentricity and the Argument for Civic Commitment: Ideology and Citizenship in a United States of Africa

MOLEFI KETE ASANTE

This article discusses an ideological framework, that is, a superstructure for continental civic commitment to African nationalism based on the perceived and practical relationships of Africans with each other. In an attempt to minimize the threats of regional, religious, or ethnic obstacles to continental integration and civic commitment to the continent, the author proposes both intellectual and pragmatic steps for continental integration. Using concrete examples, as well as generative source philosophies, myths, and traditional proverbs as fundamentals for the creation of a new ethic of politics, this article seeks to advance a deeper perspective on continental citizenship.

Keywords: Afrocentricity; civic commitment; ideology; citizenship

I am interested in exploring ways to advance the integration of the African continent. My method of analysis and my proposal for civic commitment are based on an extensive survey of African history from its ancient times—the emergence of United Kemet under the leadership of Mena the Conqueror—to the creation of the African Union (AU) in 2002. This time frame—from 3400 BCE to 2002 CE—constitutes the longest period of continuous civilization in human history, one that provides us with numerous examples and illustrations of Afrocentricity.

When I wrote the book *The History of Africa* (Asante 2007), I focused on African activities

Molefi Kete Asante is a professor in the Department of African American Studies at Temple University. He is a guest professor at Zhejiang University, Hangzhou, China. He has published 70 books, among the most recent of which are Maulana Karenga: An Intellectual Portrait *(Polity 2009);* Afrocentric Manifesto *(Polity 2008); and* The History of Africa: The Quest for Eternal Harmony *(Routledge 2007). In 2002 he received the distinguished Douglas Ehninger Award for Rhetorical Scholarship from the National Communication Association. He is a regular consultant to the African Union. He is the founding editor of the* Journal of Black Studies.

DOI: 10.1177/0002716210378569

ANNALS, *AAPSS*, 632, November 2010
121

from the standpoint of Africans as agents of progress, change, development, science, art, religion, and politics. Later, with Ama Mazama, I coedited the *Encyclopedia of African Religion* (Asante and Mazama 2008), with the express purpose of discovering Africa's most fundamental thoughts on a range of issues, including human behavior, the role of the divine, and human will. In addition, I have followed the arguments and logic of Pan-Africanism from its inception to its contemporary manifestations in the works of Cheikh Tidiane Gadio, Muammar al-Qaddafi, and others. This article is an extension of such work in which I mold the knowledge that I have inherited from these studies and from the people who have taught me to provide a framework for a civil society based on the simple idea of viewing Africans as agents of history, not marginal to European or Arabian histories, but central to our own historical experiences. Without such a universal African sense of exceptionalism within the context of our own history, land, and activities, it will be nearly impossible for Africans to overcome the numerous obstacles that stand in the way of a continental state. The requirements for a continental civil society begin with common reasons and emotions about who Africans are on the continent and in our diaspora.

The Pan-African Dream

Africa's Pan-African dream since the 1884–1885 Berlin Conference sponsored by Kaiser Wilhelm, Bismarck, and King Leopold has been for the unity of the African continent. Fourteen European nations met, without Africans, from November to February during that winter in Germany to divide what they considered to be "a magnificent cake" between their countries. What emerged from these imperial conferees were three important doctrines that would govern European political and military policies toward Africa for more than a century. These were defined as follows:

> *The doctrine of the spheres of influence* by which Europe established its right to control the African coastline.
> *The doctrine of effective occupation* by which Europe established the idea that it could occupy an entire country by controlling the commerce along the coast.
> *The doctrine of European protection of its agents*, especially missionaries, explorers, and scientists who exploited the African people's resources.

Resistance and Independence

Despite Europe's attempt to impose absolute hegemony on Africa, Africans resisted and created organizations that made Europe's occupation imperfect and very difficult. After the independence of Egypt and Ghana in 1952 and 1957, respectively, the call for African unity increased at the level of African leadership. Gamel Nasser of Egypt, Haile Selassie of Ethiopia, and Kwame Nkrumah of Ghana pushed for the creation of the Organization of African Unity (OAU). The organization had two purposes: (1) freeing the continent from colonial domination and (2) creating an African state. The first objective was met, but the OAU could not meet the second objective.

Indeed, revolutionaries took up arms in many regions of the continent to fight against the colonial powers. In other regions, although less militaristic, the people used boycotts, demonstrations, and work stoppages to make the occupation of the continent impossible. In the end, the entire continent expelled the colonial menace. We experienced self-government again and dreamed of a united Africa. Thus, the African Union (formerly the OAU) has revitalized the dream of millions of Africa's children for a civil society based on the values and virtues of our traditions.

Ensuring Civic Commitment to a Continental State

I aim to demonstrate several operational strategies and tactics for achieving a civic commitment that will equip Africa's civil society with a set of principles and aspirations that can be shared by the entire population. This can be achieved only with turn-key—opening and engaging—elements that make things happen.

Thus, the major question that I want to answer is, "How do we ensure the civic commitment of a diverse population of African peoples to national integration?" Put another way, "How can African peoples become *the* African people?"

The answers to these questions reside in an ideological structure that must be historically discovered, culturally maintained, and politically buttressed by the masses of African people. It cannot be something imposed from above but must be found in the authentic lives of the people as they maintain their own sense of dignity. In the *Afrocentric Manifesto* I argued that agency was a key attribute of the movement toward African renaissance (Asante 2008).

African culture tends to be open, exposed, and lived existentially across the continent. Therefore, Africans know what the obstacles are to a continental nationalism, and they have the courage and the will to confront those obstacles.

Obstacles to National Integration

I do not need to spend time reiterating the obstacles to continental unity, but I will list the principal debating points in the interest of all of us sharing the same page in the book: *regionalism, ethnic chauvinism*, and *religious faith*. Cynics often cite these areas as great stumbling blocks to continental unity. I happen to be of the opinion that what can connect us is far greater and stronger than what can divide us. You might say that I am a firm believer in the idea of Africa in the same way that Garvey, Diop, Nkrumah, and others saw it: as the best possibility for humanity because the values that are found among the African masses have rarely been integrated into Africa's political deliberations and institutions (Mazama 2003). Ngugi has said, "To control a people's culture is to control their tools of self-determination" (Thiong'o 1986, 16). Bekerie (1994) has also established the fundamental basis for an Afrocentric view of the African reality. Once Africans claim their own national consciousness from the peoples' liberation struggles, we will have regained our civic footing. Our history is full of the proper stories and symbols of achievement. What did we fight for but our land, our right to self-governance, and the right of all humans to be treated with dignity, which is the very element that protects our commitment to diversity (Asante 1998)?

Characteristics of Civic Commitment

The ideological configuration of the African citizen in a continental state is distinguished by seven characteristics found in the most successful African societies, such as Ancient Kemet during the eighteenth dynasty under the Kamosians, the Ghanaian Empire that lasted for 1,500 years from 300 BCE until it was overthrown by Sundiata in 1242 CE, the Monomotapa Kingdom that built hundreds of stone cities in the south of the continent, and the fabled Kingdom of Axum of the seventh through the tenth centuries. Other examples are too numerous to mention but are just as important in the restructuring of our historiography, as I will demonstrate.

The seven characteristics of a continental civil society include the following:

1. *Civic promotion of African culture:* There must be an active and genuine promotion of African culture as determined by symbols, motifs, rituals, education, scripts, proverbs, and ceremonies.

The establishment of the United States of Africa will demand that people give allegiance to a much larger community than they have ever realized. This is true even though Europeans regularly consider all Africans to be of one country. We are at the historic crossroads where this has to become the African reality. A promotion of African culture from the simplest institutions to the most complex must be Africans' objective every day. The state, therefore, must have at its disposal the most active propaganda cadre to affirm the value of African symbols, rituals, scripts, and so forth that enrich the lives of the people and bring Africans together as one nation. If we examine the problems of disunity in any one of the states inherited from the Berlin Conference, we see that the source is often lack of proper appreciation of common objectives and consequently the minimizing of the roles of others. Every person in a continental African state must have his or her dignity protected; this should be the fundamental core of the political and juridical system.

2. *Attachment to the subject place of Africans:* There must be an emotional attachment to the subject place of Africans in any social, political, economic, architectural, literary, or religious phenomenon with implications for gender and class consideration.

This characteristic is clearly meant to produce a citizenry ready to defend its homeland. No one should be permitted to marginalize any African in any situation. Africans' collective response to being placed on the periphery of world history must be total rejection of that position. There is a sense that some Asians, Europeans, and Americans are comfortable with a weak Africa because it means a weak African people. This is no longer acceptable. We must have a belief that we are in the center of our own history. Let us begin with new maps of the world that place Africa in the center of the world. This is what every nation does anyway. So let cartographers produce what we need to teach the children of Africa. Let us create universities that are Afrocentric, not Eurocentric, where the central narrative from the past to the future is Africa. This means that the column of information standing at the center of the hypostyle hall of knowledge in most African universities should no longer be headed by Socrates; Plato; Aristotle; Pythagoras; Julius Caesar; Mary, Queen of Scots; Henry, the Navigator; Goethe; Dante; and so forth. Maulana Karenga's insistence of a moral narrative, based on the best principles of the African classical past, should take a central place in the development of all curricula in Africa (Karenga 2002).

We must impose our own knowledge at the center of our educational system. African children must know Imhotep; Amenhotep, the son of Hapu; Duauf; Akhenaten; Hannibal; Hatshepsut; Hanno, the Sailor; Thutmoses III; Amadu Bamba; Wole Soyinka; Ngugi wa Thiong'o; Nzingha; Nehanda; Langston Hughes; DuBois; Diop; Fanon; Menelik II; Sungbo's Eredo; Nagast; and so forth.

There is no history and there have been no men or women any greater than the geniuses produced on this continent. There are no places any more sacred than those that have been hallowed by the deeds and presence of our own ancestors (Asante 2007). Marcus Garvey is often cited as saying that "the white man has out-propagandized us" (Garvey 1986, 234). What he meant was that the narrative of Africa was not written by Africans but by Europeans or, we might add, by Arabs, whose objectives were not the same as those of the African people that they had conquered.

Let our universities have students who come from lower schools that teach the greatness of our collective history. African men and women who have achieved a place in our memory because of their deeds must be shown to be those who believed in the centrality of Africans to their own narratives.

3. *Defense of African cultural elements:* There must be an active defense of African cultural elements as historically valid in the context of art, music, education, science, and literature.

African citizens' civic commitment must be to the ideal African cultural elements. If you study art, education, science, literature, philosophy, or mathematics, first interrogate it from the standpoint of African culture (Asante 2008). African *sebayet*, or proverbs, must be reintroduced as the cornerstone of our cultural communication. It should be said at some point in time, if we are good politicians and teachers and philosophers, that our masses understand the comprehensive nature of our *sebayet*. We must not be stuck in the past, but we must not forget the past; we must use it as a resource to ensure civic commitment and to build our civil society.

What I am proposing is that the educators interrogate the most ancient documents as well as the epics, myths, and narratives of Africa to discover the wisdom that we have inherited. This is not to reject useful information from other sources but, rather, to ensure that in the national community Africans use all of the available knowledge in the world, beginning with that produced by our own thinkers and sages. Others do this and celebrate their philosophers; we are no less than others (Zulu 1999). The names of Imhotep, Merikare, and Khunanup must become commonplace among the masses.

4. *Celebration of centeredness:* There must be a celebration of "centeredness" and agency and an uncompromising commitment to lexical refinement that eliminates pejoratives about Africans.

Our intention must be to reshape language so that all negativity, gathered for 500 years, against Africa and Africans is destroyed. This is a national citizenship drive. We must assume that we can eliminate negative references to Africans as we can eliminate a fly. We can start with the youth to work to obliterate all traces of negativity about Africa. They must see themselves in the service of something far greater than their own immediate lives. They must celebrate centeredness by dreaming of greatness for the nation. Terminology associated with Africa such as "primitive," "traditional," "ethnic," "Pygmy," and "Hottentot" must be abandoned as part of this national effort to affirm African dignity (Karenga 2002, 23–100). It is true that this continent has the earliest human beings, the earliest civilizations, but there are no "primitives" in this land. An effort to eradicate the definitions imposed on Africa by Europe should be a primary goal of the civil society. Our music, religion, dance, and families need no qualifying adjectives that leave Europeans as an imposed universal. Their dance is as *ethnic* as ours. Their music is as *traditional* as ours. Their religion is no more valid than ours. We are all humans, and the role of the civil society in an integrated continental nation must be to drive out all forces that would make Africans and blackness pejorative.

5. *Revising the collective text:* There must be a powerful imperative from innovative research institutions to revise the collective text of African people.

Our children must reject notions of African inferiority. I was asked by a 16-year-old girl at an elite school in West Africa, "What would have happened to Africa if the whites had not come?" I said to her that we would have been much further along than we are now and we would have not suffered the same psychological and cultural upheavals that we now have. During the days before the invaders we were able to leave all doors unlocked; now that we have had Western civilization we have to double-lock our doors. Africa would not have been a continent so severely maligned. While we escaped the decimation of the natives of Australia, New Zealand, and the Americas, we became disoriented with the persistence of the physical, cultural, and economic violence against our people.

6. *Acceptance of African diversity:* There must be a massive acceptance of Africa as "the nation that embraces diversity."

Africans must create the educational and cultural mechanism that will deliver the national message that Africa embraces diversity. In a nation that has nearly 2,000 languages and numerous nationalities, kingdoms, and empires, it is un-African to oppose diversity. All modern nations are diverse; Africa will be no less diverse by virtue of its unity. Those who argue that unification will flatten Africa's diversity are rarely those who care about the vigorous integration of the continent. However, integration cannot be directed by any particular leading element or ethnicity. Indeed, to claim that any one element of this vast nation is its leading edge is to practice provincialism. This acceptance of diversity means that there should be respect for the historic ancestors of every ethnic and linguistic group that defines itself as African. There are no superior and inferior ethnic communities in Africa. Such an idea, if it exists, is merely a false notion imported from outside of our continent.

Africa has the opportunity to serve as a standard for "the nation that embraces diversity," for the twenty-first century and beyond. In fact, as Africans we have the opportunity to assert a narrative of the future filled with human freedom and possibilities. This narrative contains a message of leadership; this is not Africa waiting for others to define the Millennium, the New World Order, or the Era of Assistance Fatigue, or reacting to the Group of Twenty. No, this is Africa taking the initiative to define itself as a society that embraces diversity.

7. *Openness to the diaspora:* There must be an openness to include all of the achievements and contributions of African people as the collective gift of Africa to humanity.

The African nation, as a continent, is simply the core of a much larger African world. Those of us who were born outside of the continent and reside in thousands of places around the globe must be seen, as most of us see ourselves, as adding to the flow of African life. We have moved or been forced away, but we have never been detached from the continent. Our poets have sung brilliantly of Africa in Jamaica, Haiti, Colombia, Costa Rica, Trinidad, Guadeloupe, Brazil, Suriname, Venezuela, Puerto Rico, Cuba, Uruguay, Ecuador, Peru, the United States, Canada, and islands too numerous to mention. It is not just that every time we look at ourselves, we see the imprint of Africa; it is also that our emotional and psychological attachments to the motherland have never been severed regardless of the brutality that Africans have suffered.

The richness of the diaspora in every kind of human achievement is an extension of the richness of Africa. We are African products, however mangled by circumstances and however misguided by Africa's enemies, and as Africans we count our weaknesses and our wealth as African weaknesses and wealth. When we celebrate Arnaldo Tamayo and Guion Bluford—the first two Africans to fly in space, one as a cosmonaut from Cuba and the other as an astronaut from the United States—because they declared their Africanness, we celebrate ourselves. Their achievements must be placed alongside all other African achievements. What others have done, we can do; what others wish to do, we have done. This is the African condition.

As in previous ages, our inventors have added to the stock of human knowledge. When the sages of our villages and towns created new ways to deal with lingering technical problems, they were adding to the Pan-African repertoire of creations. Multiply the activity of men and women in science thousands of times over and you have the creative energy of human beings who made it possible for African communities to have farming instruments and implements of war. But these are not the only areas of creativity among our people. We have given to the world superior artists, creative novelists, competitive athletes in all sports, wise philosophers, incomparable engineers and space scientists, gifted mathematicians, impressive sailors who have rounded the earth alone, noble historians, and unselfish politicians. The grand names of our military leaders—Mena, Thutmoses III, Ramses II, Hannibal, Nana Karikari, Yenenga, Nzingha, Shaka, Toussaint L'Ouverture, Dessalines, Nanny, Nat Turner, Sundiata, Prudencio, Mzilikazi, Lat Dior, Zumbi, and a thousand others—must be resurrected and remembered by our own historians. We must now embrace our mutual heritage and claim the entirety of our African nationality.

These seven bases for national unity function to move Africa toward a common nationalistic agenda. Unification is the only way to reduce and minimize national antagonisms and regional disputes based upon stereotypes and false images of others. If Africans take it as their responsibility to protect the least among them—the smallest ethnic units, the most threatened languages, the people nearest the brink of destitution—we will advance a new ethic in the historical book of life.

Explain the Functions

The unity of Africa is a necessity for the recovery and maintenance of African dignity. What will constitute the substantive ingredients for a common body polity?

What metaphor for the literal state will emerge as the national instrument for what the philosopher Maulana Karenga calls "dignity-affirming integration" (Asante 2009)? What shall we say about the African lion? How shall its deepest character be announced in ways that produce in citizens a sense of togetherness, community, and shared destiny? These are the issues, along with the nuts and bolts of the political system, that must be managed if Africa is to build a civic commitment.

The control of African resources is essential for a free Africa and a continent in quest for the narrative of the future. Thus, economic unity and economic freedom walk hand in hand. If we encourage massive creative thinking in terms of the continent, we will generate billions for the renaissance and regeneration of the continent. Imagine a young woman who seeks to make a name for herself in business gaining a loan from the African National Bank to build textile factories in Casablanca, Nairobi, and Cape Town. She would travel and see the extent of the vast nation, learning all of the time about the history and development of the continent. Our resistance to hegemonic intrusion and the attempt at recolonization of Africa will be marked by our unyielding commitment to our civil society as evidenced by our moral, legal, and economic defense of the homeland. We can have a broad civic commitment to a national civil society and also have a microscopic spotlight on each local community.

Turn-Key Strategies

We must engage in persistent and consistent campaigns that emphasize the value of Pan-Africanism as a viable strategy for obtaining Afrocentric solidarity. Pan-Africanism, without a commitment to Africa's best interest, is without energy and without a thriving ideological focus. To say, "I am a Pan-Africanist," and not to work in the interest of the agency of Africans, is to abuse the term "Pan-African." I contend that just being African is sufficient to capture the essence of Pan-Africanism.

To be African is to believe in two overarching constructs: a narrative of the future and the idea of a nation embracing diversity.

The narrative of the future must engage every civil servant in the continental African nation. Each person must be involved in bringing into existence this comprehensive view of the nation. We will need playwrights to write plays and pageants that employ the ancient and traditional rituals and ceremonies to elevate the national state in the minds of the masses. Old enemies and sectional rivals must be in the same play, the same ritual, the same ceremony. Where we have heard negative stereotypes of our neighbors, we must have institutions that encourage unity. To do so, our civil institutions must create awards and incentives for those who work toward the political and emotional integration of the nation. Why not institute a series of $50,000-a-year awards to honor those citizens who best demonstrate their commitment to one of the seven elements necessary for national integration?

Civil bureaucracies might create contests for the best ideas for integrating in each state national agricultural methods and knowledge. There might also be elaborate university scholarships to students who best articulate in research papers the ideas contained in the documents of a national state. Why should not the national intelligentsia be encouraged to produce works that respond to the African condition rather than to the situations in the West? Reward structures must be redirected toward the continent and away from the West so that our scientists will solve the problems of the African state. Nothing should stand in the way of Africans' commitment to a civil society that is collectively engaged in uplifting the African people.

A commitment to diversity is central to the advancement of the civil society, and this means that all forms of ethnic chauvinism should be pursued to the extent of the law and punished so as to dictate by law the idea that Africa is the nation that embraces diversity.

One way to achieve this collective civil society is through photographs of different races, religions, and ethnic groups among Africans. These posters, whether manually created or digitally established, might be useful in all sectors of the society where civil servants are being recruited. Consultants who are skilled in diversity education might be employed to teach those who are already employed by their individual states, once the continental state is created. Nothing should block the promotion of the narrative of the future and the motto of the nation as one that embraces diversity. Every institution in the state must be so dedicated to these overarching ideas that all citizens are daily reminded of the constituents of unity. Where other nations in the world may not have a narrative of the future, Africa will. Where other nations may not embrace diversity, Africa must. We operationalize, that is, make this happen, by introducing turn-key activities that engage the citizens in a commitment to the civil society. For example, all science teaching, from the earliest grades in school through universities, must cast Africa as the nation of the future. Children must be encouraged to study scenarios for the future in the sciences. They must be allowed to ask, "What if?" This is the only way that we will be able to leapfrog the difficulties encountered in the West and the rest of the world. Technological problems that the West has encountered do not have to be engaged in by an African population that embraces new forms of economic and social development. We do not need to go through the same steps as others (Akinyela 1996). Africa must not follow the path of polluting the seas, destroying the rainforests, or supporting runaway exploitation of the earth's resources.

He who is against diversity is against the idea of Africa. He who has distaste for his fellow African on the basis of ethnic, religious, or regional feelings is an enemy of the continental African state. The unified state is the only path to our true destiny. Children of Africa, hear us today. Listen to our voices and take up your computers, your pens, your agricultural tools, your engineering instruments, and your books, and walk proudly toward the future with one goal, one aim, one destiny, as one people. Nothing is stronger, nor more correct, than Africa's commitment to a new civil society. Teach it, study it, embrace it, and rejoice because you have found your family on the continent and in the diaspora, and they are coming together with a bond that cannot be broken again by betrayal, ignorance, and greed. We are on the road to resurrect Africa in the image of Africa.

References

Akinyela, Makungu Mshairi. 1996. Black families, cultural democracy and self-determination: An African centered pedagogy. PhD diss., Pacific Oaks College, Pasadena, CA.

Asante, Molefi Kete. 1998. *The Afrocentric idea*. Rev. and expanded ed. Philadelphia, PA: Temple University Press.

Asante, Molefi Kete. 2007. *The history of Africa: The quest for eternal harmony*. London, UK: Routledge.

Asante, Molefi Kete. 2008. *An Afrocentric manifesto*. Cambridge, UK: Polity.

Asante, Molefi Kete. 2009. *Maulana Karenga: An intellectual portrait*. Cambridge, UK: Polity.

Asante, Molefi Kete, and Ama Mazama, eds. 2008. *Encyclopedia of African religion*. Thousand Oaks, CA: SAGE.

Bekerie, Ayele. 1994. The 4 corners of a circle: Afrocentricity as a model of synthesis. *Journal of Black Studies* 25 (2): 131–49.

Garvey, Marcus. 1986. *The philosophy and Opinions of Marcus Garvey*, ed. Amy J. Garvey. Dover, MA: Majority Press.

Karenga, Maulana. 2002. *Introduction to black studies*. Los Angeles, CA: University of Sankore Press.

Mazama, Ama, ed. 2003. *The Afrocentric paradigm*. Trenton, NJ: Africa World Press.

Thiong'o, Ngugi wa. 1986. *Decolonising the mind: The politics of language in African literature*. London, UK: Heinemann.

Zulu, Itibari M. 1999. Exploring the African centered paradigm: Discourse and innovation in African world community studies. Los Angeles, CA: Amen-Ra Theological Seminary Press.

ERRATUM

Bradburn, Norman M. and Carolyn J. E. Fuqua. 2010. Indicators and the Federal Statistical System: An Essential but Fraught Partnership. *The Annals of the American Academy of Political and Social Science* 631:89–108.

In this article, Carolyn J. E. Fuqua's name was misspelled in the reference list. The correct reference should appear as:

Fuqua, Carolyn J. E. 2010. The most intimate collaboration: Business interests and the development of U.S. official statistics. PhD. diss., University of Chicago.

DOI: 10.1177/0002716210385213